cha

Peter J. Sn...

The Pet Parrot Book

With photographs by Alex Bellotti,
Lisa Zingsheim, and Joan Balzarini

Illustrations by Michelle Earle-Bridges

BARRON'S

Dedication

For Andrew M. Snyder, M.D., my brother, whom I love and respect more than anyone can equal.

Cover Photos

Animals Animals: Front cover; Joan Balzarini: Back cover top, bottom; inside front cover, inside back cover.

Photo Credits

Lisa Zingsheim: page 6; Joan Balzarini: pages viii, 23, 40, 47, 65; all other photos by Alex Bellotti.

Copyright 1998 by Peter J. Snyder and the Philip Lief Group, Inc.
Developed by the Philip Lief Group, Inc.

All inquiries should be addressed to:
Barron's Educational Series, Inc.
250 Wireless Boulevard
Hauppauge, New York 11788

http://www.barronseduc.com

Library of Congress Catalog Card No. 98-4264

International Standard Book No. 0-7641-0608-2

Library of Congress Cataloging-in-Publication Data

Snyder, Peter J., 1964–
    The pet parrot book : the complex relationship between humans and their parrots / by Peter J. Snyder ; photographs by Alex Bellotti.
        p.   cm. — (A pet reference book)
    Includes bibliographical references (p. 94) and index.
    ISBN 0-7641-0608-2
    1. Parrots. 2. Pet owners. 3. Human-animal relationships.
I. Title. II. Title.
SF473.P3S59   1998
636.6′865—dc21   98-4264
                              CIP

Printed in Hong Kong

987654321

The Author

Peter J. Snyder, Ph.D. is Director of the Division of Behavior Neurology, Department of Neurology, Allegheny General Hospital, Pittsburgh, Pennsylvania. His work there encompasses diagnosing and treating patients with various brain disorders that may effect their speech, memory, behavior, comprehension, or other thought process. Dr. Snyder has been studying complex relationships between behavior, cognition, and the structure and function of the brain since entering graduate school in 1986. He is also an associate professor of neurology at MCP ◆ Hahnemann School of Medicine, Allegheny University of the Health Sciences. A longtime parrot lover and owner, Dr. Snyder combines his passion for parrots with his research at the National Aviary in Pittsburgh.

The National Aviary was awarded this title by an act of Congress and President Clinton. It is the nation's only free-standing indoor-outdoor facility that is wholly dedicated to avian exhibition, education, conservation, and research.

A percentage of all royalties from the sale of this book are donated in support of the research and worldwide conservation projects of The National Aviary.

Important Note

The author and publisher consider it important to emphasize that the advice given in this book is meant primarily for normally developed, healthy parrots from a reliable breeder or supplier. Poorly socialized or unhealthy parrots may be a danger to the well-being of other pets and humans in the household.

Anyone who acquires an adult parrot should be aware that the bird has already formed its basic impressions of humans. Before taking the bird home, the new owner should watch the parrot carefully, including its behavior toward humans, and should meet the previous owner if possible.

Outdoor release or unrestricted outdoor flight of parrots is absolutely condemned by the ethical parrot owner. The book recommends that parrot wing feathers be carefully trimmed regularly.

Table of Contents

Preface   vi

Introduction   1

1. Parrots and Mankind: A Venerable Relationship   3
   Early Classes   3
   The History of Bird Keeping   5
   Poaching Rings   6
   Australia's "Pests"   8
   Endangered Parrots   8

2. A Parrot, or Two, or Fifty, in Your Household   12
   Social Animals   12
   Diets in Captivity   15
   Protecting Your Parrot   16
   Choosing Life with a Parrot   21

3. Sex and the Single Parrot   25
   Your Parrot's True Nature   25
   Parrots Love Routine   26
   The Importance of Companionship   26
   Pair-Bonding   27
   Sexual Maturation and Behavioral Change   29
   Parrot Societies and Your Living Room   29
   Breeding for Survival   30

4. Parrots and Four-Legged Companions   32
   Sharing Food and Company   32
   Kittens and Parrots   34
   Introducing the Animals   35

5. A Parrot's Cage Is Its Castle   37
Where to Put the Cage   37
Temperature and Humidity   39
Choosing a Cage Design   40
Cage Bedding   42
Toys and Swings   42
Cleaning and Hygiene   43
Baths and Showers   44
Air Quality   44
Lighting   45

6. I'll Eat Almost Anything   47
The Omnivorous Parrot   47
Safe Foods   49
Food Preparation and Time Management   51
Reforming the "Seed Junkie"   51
Vitamin and Mineral Supplements   52

7. A Watchful Eye on Sickness and Disease   54
Preventive Medicine   54
Follow These Rules to Good Health   54
The Early Warning Signs of Illness   55
Bacterial, Viral, and Parasitic Illnesses   57
Hazards in the Home   59
Care and Grooming   60
Feather Plucking   63

8. Establishing the Pecking Order   65
Introducing Your Parrot to Its New Home   65
Your Parrot's Body Language   67
Bringing Up Baby   68
What if My Bird Bites?   69
Spoiling Baby   71
How Do I Stop the Screaming?   72
Stopping Problems before They Start   73

9. Training Your Bird to Talk   75
Language or Memory?   75
Which Parrots Are the Best Talkers?   77
Which Parrots Respond Best to Training?   78

How Large Can a Parrot's Vocabulary Get?   80
Which Training Techniques Work Best?   81

10.   What Parrots Can Teach Us About Ourselves   84
What Is Intelligence?   84
Perception and Expression of Emotion   85
Limb Preference (Footedness)   87
Parrot and Human Brain Asymmetries   87
The Future of Parrots and Humans   89

Glossary   91

Useful Addresses and Literature   94

Index   95

Preface

The Parrot has watched Man in his folly the way he watched the Brontosaurus devour the trees—with curiosity. But man has stuck it out longer on the planet than the Thunder Lizard did, and the Parrot has developed a tolerant affection for the two-footed, wingless idiot whose record of prolonged calamity we call history.

—John Phillips, *Dear Parrot*
London: J.M. Dent & Sons Ltd.
1980, p. 54

I am a neuropsychologist—someone who is trained as a cross between a clinical psychologist and a neurologist. My job is to diagnose and treat patients in hospitals who have all sorts of brain disorders that affect their ability to think clearly, speak, understand language, remember things, or behave appropriately. Since entering graduate school in 1986, I have been fortunate to have had several excellent teachers, as well as wonderful opportunities to engage in research to better define the complex relationships among behavior, cognition, and the structure and function of the brain.

When I started graduate school and moved to East Lansing, Michigan in 1986, my girlfriend bought me my first bird, a cockatiel, so that I wouldn't be lonely. This initial $45 purchase turned out to be a very wise investment, as this small animal brought an enormous amount of pleasure into my life. Although, unfortunately, my cockatiel died eight years later, due to a difficult-to-treat bone infection, she opened up a world to me that I am still excited by and continually learning about. So, it was back in 1986 that both my research career, and what my family might call an obsession with parrots, both began.

Most people have a hard time finding ways to mix their professional careers with their hobbies or leisure interests. That's a tough problem, and it took ten years before I came up with a solution. After spending this past decade trying to better understand how the human nervous system grows in such a way as to cause strong preferences for the use of one side of the body or the other for motor functions—handedness—my mentor in graduate school pointed something out to me: Parrots might be the single best animal model for studying human handedness. In fact, the first reports suggesting that parrots might teach us a lot about human handedness date back to 1647 . . . nearly 350 years ago. This meant that I could study the motor behaviors (physical activity) of parrots, and possibly learn more about handedness in humans, than if I studied any other type of animal—including nonhuman primates such as chimpanzees. This was the "hook" I'd been searching for; I had found a way to combine my scientific research with my personal interest in parrots; and, this is precisely what I've done.

The author with Congo African Grey. Green Wing Macaw in background.

Acknowledgments

I would not have been able to write this book if my mentor and good friend, Professor Lauren Julius Harris, had not opened up this area of research interest to me while I was his graduate student. In 1989 he authored what is now considered to be the definitive article on the history of research on motor asymmetries (footedness) in parrots, and it was this paper that first pointed me in the right direction (see Useful Addresses and Literature, page 94).

I am also very fortunate to enjoy the support and encouragement of both the Executive Director, Dayton Baker, and his entire highly skilled staff at the National Aviary in Pittsburgh. Both Dayton and his Curator of Birds, Jim Bonner, have welcomed me into the flock at the National Aviary—as both a member of its International Scientific Advisory Board, and as a member of the Institutional Animal Care and Use Committee (IACUC). As the only free-standing aviary—that is, not connected to a larger zoo—in North America, the National Aviary is truly a national treasure. It is with the financial and logistical support of this remarkable institution that I am able to pursue research that attempts to bridge the seemingly disparate areas of parrot behavior and neurobiology with human brain functioning and behavior. Additionally, the support of my research assistant, Mrs. Nicole A. Ceravolo-Begg has been, and continues to

Parrots may hold the key to discovery of human brain functions.

be, invaluable to me—thank you. My mother, Susan J. Etkind, is the most supportive, caring, and wise parent that anyone could hope for. My fiancee, Amy Laura Feldman, M.D., could always make me smile whenever I worried about writing and editing deadlines. I must also thank the Department of Neurology at the Allegheny Campus of the MCP ◆ Hahnemann School of Medicine, and particularly my chairman, Jon Brillman, M.D., for the freedom to pursue questions that are at least on the fringe, if not the cutting edge, of comparative neurology.

Introduction

This book is a natural extension of a large survey study, which I conducted in 1995, of parrot owners who live throughout North America, Great Britain, Europe, Australia, and New Zealand. I sent questionnaires to owners of parrots about their birds' age, sex, living conditions, vocalization ability—(meaning the actual size of each parrot's lexicon of human speech sounds)—and foot preference. This questionnaire was sent to many parrot clubs, posted to a discussion group (rec.pets.birds) on the Internet, and published in the September 1995 issue of *Bird Talk* magazine. I was pleased to receive a great response to this survey, and many people were also kind enough to share funny stories, photographs, poems, and drawings about their cherished avian family members.

Although these responses were great fun to receive, they posed a problem for me that I hadn't anticipated. Specifically, funny stories don't mix well with the dry, technical, scientific papers that I had anticipated writing as a result of conducting this study. Of course, the articles for scientific journals need to be written, but how could I simply file away in my basement a large box of wonderful letters that parrot owners from around the world graciously wrote in answer to my request? It was this particular problem that led to the idea for this book.

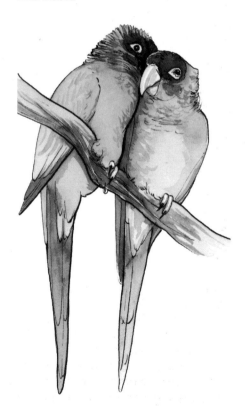

With this book I want to share my thoughts, concerns, and advice about living with companion parrots in our homes, as well as to provide an outlet for sharing (anonymously) some of the funny stories and observations offered by hundreds of parrot owners. There is no way to include stories from each person who was kind enough to participate in my survey but I have hopefully edited a collection of these comments and observations that will both amuse and inform the reader. I have tried to insert these contributions where appropriate throughout the book as I wind my way from topic to topic—offering my own advice and observations on the proper care of parrots, from both scientific and personal perspectives. A good friend, veterinary technician and parrot breeder, Lisa Zingsheim, has graciously provided her own valuable advice in helping me to prepare the chapter on diet and nutrition (Chapter Six).

This book is intended for those of us lucky enough to already share our homes with a parrot or two (or three, or four . . .), and for others who are considering for the first time this wonderful way of life and serious commitment. If you fall into this latter group, I will provide important issues to consider *before* you choose to drastically modify your lifestyle by accepting the responsibility of caring for a parrot. For those of you who have already made this choice, I will provide ideas and information that might assist you in better understanding your companion's behavior, intellectual prowess, and lovable eccentricities. Most of the information I present is derived from my own experience as a parrot owner for nearly 15 years, and from my informal education in avian biology and behavior. I am not an ornithologist by training, and so certain points I make might not be completely accurate . . . but I have tried my best to keep this to a minimum. This book is not intended for readers who are interested in the breeding of parrots or the raising of very young birds that have not yet been weaned. At the end of this book I have listed a few sources of information (see page 94) that have done a better job than I possibly could at providing crucial information on these topics.

Chapter One

Parrots and Mankind: A Venerable Relationship

Early Classes

Birds have always held an esteemed position as unchallenged masters of the skies, dating back to their presumed first appearance on earth, in the Upper Jurassic Period, approximately 150,000,000 years ago. Although they probably originated with the reptilelike yet warm blooded, feather-winged *archaeopteryx*, over the millennia their bodies have adapted away from their more reptilian ancestors in order to better adopt a life of flight. Although they did not evolve concurrently with dinosaurs, as suggested by the fanciful quote by John Phillips in the Preface, modern birds are thought to have descended from one of two ancestral groups of archosaurs—the other being the crocodilians—which in turn descended from an earlier class of animals termed Reptilia. This early class also included families of animals that gave rise to modern turtles, snakes, and lizards. For the earliest birds, in the class of archosaurs that also included the dinosaurs, many scientists believe that the reptilian scales evolved into feathers to support flight, and very important internal skeletal changes accompanied the development of wings and flight muscles. The dinosaurs suffered extinction toward the end of the Mesozoic Era, which ended approximately 100 million years ago, but the class Aves (birds) have survived as their closest living relatives.

Archaeopteryx (which means "ancient wing") made its first

Fossil remains of Archaeopteryx.

reptile, with a long bony tail, needle-sharp claws, and a mouth full of teeth. In fact, the ancestors of modern birds held on to their teeth until about 75 million years ago; however, new archaeological evidence suggests that there may have been at least one other line of birdlike creatures that gave up their teeth for a beak long before the ancestors of our modern birds did. Recently, paleontologists from the Chinese Academy of Sciences in Beijing reported the discovery of an early birdlike animal, *Confuciusornis sanctus*, which made its first appearance in northeastern China about 142 million years ago. What is remarkable about this finding is that this early bird had a toothless beak. In all likelihood, *Confuciusornis* was not the ancestor of today's birds, which, of course, all have beaks, as other features of its head, arms, and body suggest that it belonged to a class of birds called enantiornithines ("opposite birds"). These animals most likely vanished with the dinosaurs about 65 million years ago. However, the discovery of *Confuciusornis* indicates that beaks may have arisen as an evolutionary adaptation in two very different groups of birds that seemingly had no physical contact with each other. A life of flight in early birds led to strong evolutionary pressures to develop a lightweight beak.

appearance in Europe about 147 million years ago, in the geographical region now occupied by Germany. This proto-bird resembled a

At any rate, we currently believe that our companion parrots are direct descendants of *Archaeopteryx*, and along with the turtle and the alligator, they are one of the few living direct reminders of the Age of the Dinosaurs. Unlike the alligator, however, our modern birds have changed considerably in physical design from their Upper Jurassic Period ancestors. Most of their scales (except those on their legs and feet) have been traded for feathers, and their whole body design and internal organ systems have been exquisitely reconfigured for life in the skies.

The History of Bird Keeping

Birds are not mammals, and their evolutionary history over the past 150 million years has been remarkably different from ours. Genetically, we have much less in common with our avian companions than we do with our cats and dogs, and yet, until very recently, our coexistence with birds on this planet has been peaceful and often mutually beneficial. Birds were initially domesticated as a source of food, as in the case of fowl, or else as a means of procuring food, as in the case of various species of falcons. Still, the keeping of birds for pleasure dates back to the time of the pharaohs in ancient Egypt, and parrots were considered to be articles of luxury during the Roman Empire, and sometimes bartered for slaves.

With the Renaissance and the discovery of the New World in the fifteenth century, attention was focused on the keeping of parrots, with the initial attraction being their capacity to mimic human speech. Parrots became popular pets of the noble classes in Europe, including royalty. For instance, King Henry VIII kept a talking African Grey Parrot at his palace at Hampton Court. With the turn of the nineteenth century, smaller and more easily affordable birds, such as canaries and budgerigars, became extremely popular. More recently, with the advent of commercial air travel, larger and more exotic birds have become both accessible and highly desirable as pets throughout Europe and North America.

Until recently, attempts at domestic breeding were limited and most available parrots were imported from the wild. Starting in the early 1990s, strict regulations banning the import of endangered species, and especially the Convention on International Trade in Endangered Species of Flora and Fauna (CITES), have led to a widespread interest and industry in domestic breeding for the pet trade. A total ban on the importation into the United States of endangered species of parrots listed by CITES did not take effect until 1992; however, nonstop worldwide habitat destruction is progressing at such an alarming rate that several avian species are added to the endangered species list each year. We now live with less than 70 percent of the species of birds that lived only 200 years ago.

Black Palm Cockatoo

Poaching Rings

Many poor natives of numerous developing countries make meager livings from the sale of wild-caught birds for a few pennies apiece. Often trees are cut down in order to remove the young chicks from nests, a practice that has led to a dramatic reduction in suitable nesting spots in the wild. The birds may also be taken from their nests, high up in the forest canopy, perhaps after smearing some homemade adhesive on a long stick and whacking the parrot with the sticky end. In one typical scenario, these animals are then sold to a local merchant for a tiny fraction of what the bird will eventually sell for, if it is lucky enough to survive. The merchant will then drug the bird with tequila or some other widely available sedative, tape the bird's beak shut, tie its feet with wire, and shove it along with several other birds into a cardboard tube. The tube might then be put into a wheel well of a car before being driven across the border of the United States and Mexico, for example. If two out of ten birds make it alive to pet shops located throughout the world, and sell for several hundred dollars apiece, then the entire process will have been profitable.

To be sure, the numbers of illegally imported birds have dropped considerably over the past decade, but widespread poaching continues. A single Black Palm Cockatoo might fetch $30,000 on the black market in the United States, after passing through several "middle-men."

Despite increasingly well-enforced laws prohibiting such unconscionable practices, numerous poaching rings continue to reap large profits by raping the natural treasures of developing countries. In

1993, a major news story covered the infiltration and surveillance of an organized poaching ring that had been operating for years out of Kennedy International Airport. Individuals arrested and charged with illegal poaching and importation as a result of that investigation included airline baggage handlers and security guards. This story is not the result of an isolated incident, but is a symptom of a problem that may force the wild populations of numerous rare parrot species into extinction.

As recently as 1996, there was a rash of federal court cases involving the large-scale smuggling of endangered avian species into the United States. One involved Anthony Silva, who pled guilty to numerous counts of smuggling various highly protected species into the United States. Mr. Silva pled guilty to running a smuggling operation and breaking U.S. Customs requirements from 1986 to 1991. This operation involved the illegal importation of a shipment of 50 wild-caught Hyacinth Macaws. This species is so endangered that it has been accorded the highest level of protection under the CITES wildlife treaty. It also involved shipments of Golden Conures, Blue-Throated Conures, Crimson-Bellied Conures, Yellow-shouldered Amazons, and Vinaceous Amazons. Ironically, Mr. Silva had been recognized as an international authority on parrots and parrot conservation. In fact, he had authored several books on the

topic, including *A Monograph of Endangered Parrots* (1989), in which he described the Hyacinth Macaw as being "worth its weight in gold." In a 1991 article describing the danger of extinction of wild populations of Hyacinth Macaws, published in *American Cage Bird* Magazine, Silva wrote that "unless all pressures are brought under control [such as illegal smuggling], this species may be unable to survive in the world to greet the 21st century."

Hyacinth Macaw

In another recent court case, two other individuals, William A. Wegner and Brian T. Bradley, were sentenced to prison terms of 60 and 41 months, respectively, for smuggling over $1,000,000 in protected wild cockatoo eggs into the United States from Australia. From 1983 to 1991 Wegner and Bradley, along with 13 others who were all convicted as coconspirators in this operation, traveled to Australia each year during the breeding season to remove eggs from nest sites. The eggs were smuggled into the United States in special homemade vests to prevent detection by Customs officials.

It would be easy to list more of these recent cases, but the point is that despite the best efforts of some governments that have passed domestic legislation banning the export of wild psittacines, such as Brazil, Bolivia, and Paraguay, and the adherence to the Convention on International Trade in Endangered Species of Wild Fauna and Flora (CITES) by 130 countries, including the United States, the smuggling of endangered species remains a hugely profitable business.

Australia's "Pests"

It is true that in some countries, such as Australia, large populations of parrots that we view as highly valued pets, like the Sulphur-Crested Cockatoo (*Cacatua galerita*), are considered by many to be annoying pests. Because the wild habitats of many species of Australian parrots have been vanishing as humans infringe on their territories of once undeveloped grasslands and forest, these birds have reciprocated by infringing on people's territory. In a country with more birds than humans, the result has been predictable—they are seen as pests because of their loud screaming and overall mess. Farmers have found these native birds to be even more troublesome because they destroy crops. Certain species, such as the Australian King Parrots (*Alisterus scapularis*) typically travel in large flocks and often destroy entire fruit orchards in a single day. Paradoxically, although farmers are not allowed to capture these offending birds and sell them in the domestic pet trade, they are allowed to kill them in order to protect their crops.

Until recently, Australian law forbade the importation or export of any birds. More recently, this restriction has been modified somewhat, and licensed breeders are allowed to export certain species of parrots to a very limited extent and under a strict set of conditions. In addition, the Australian government has taken steps to protect rapidly vanishing habitats for highly endangered species, and a number of aviculturists are licensed to capture and breed threatened species before they become "endangered."

Endangered Parrots

There has been an emerging trend over the past two decades, throughout the world, to learn more about the life cycles, habitat requirements, diet and nutritional needs, social lives, and breeding requirements of highly endangered species. Once these critical issues are understood for a particular species, well-organized management plans are designed to protect and increase the size of wild populations of such birds. For example, let us consider again the plight of the Hyacinth Macaw (*Anordorhynchus hyacinthinus*). Although this gentle, lovely animal was once plentiful in numbers, with a wide range that included much of Brazil, Bolivia, and Paraguay, the current population is estimated to number only between 3,000 and 5,000 animals. These remaining wild Hyacinths are found in three distinct populations, located in the rainforests of Paraguay and Brazil, in the valleys of northeastern Brazil, and in the Pantanal wetlands of Bolivia, Brazil, and Paraguay. Recently, an ambitious research and conservation project, funded by several supporting organizations such as the World Parrot Trust United States and United Kingdom, and several corporations such as Harrison Bird Diets and the Kaytee Avian Foundation, has led to modest successes in protecting at least one of these three remaining wild populations.

Range of Hyacinth Macaw

Brazil

Bolivia

Paraguay

Before

Today

Ecotourism

A relatively new and wildly popular trend in "adventure travel" has emerged, which has been termed *ecotourism*. Most all wildlife conser-

vation organizations, as well as numerous private travel companies and foreign government agencies, organize guided tours to protected ecosystems. The principle behind this movement is simple: Foreign tourists are willing to spend lots of money to travel to such locations in order to view and to photograph endangered species in the wild. By doing so, these masses of tourists are being led by experienced guides whose job it is to ensure that the local ecosystem is well managed and that erosion and actual disturbance to the local wildlife is kept to a minimum. Equally important, the tourists bring desperately needed funds, by spending money while on vacation, to local economies in often impoverished countries—to both support the establishment and maintenance of protected wildlife sanctuaries, and to support local businesses and communities. The hope is that local residents will better appreciate and protect the short-term as well as long-term economic value of their indigenous wildlife. Thus far, the positive impact of ecotourism around the world has met with mixed reviews, but clearly this trend in leisure travel has been a much-needed boon to many countries, and several foreign governments are beginning to view their remaining natural resources as commodities worth protecting in order to maintain tourism as a profitable industry.

Protecting Wild Habitats

The protection of wild habitats and populations of parrots is unquestionably imperative, and it is important to recognize that such efforts are supplemented and aided by the domestic breeding and keeping of parrots. Many species, such as the Bourke's Grass Parrot (*Neophema bourkii*), have been literally saved from the brink of extinction by wild capture and domestic breeding. There certainly are ways of supplying birds to the pet trade without endangering wild populations or brutalizing individual animals. Many, if not most, of the popular pet species are now very successfully bred in captivity, and

healthy domestic populations of many parrot species exist and are growing as a direct result of the enthusiastic efforts of both professional and amateur aviculturists. Throughout the world, from the Amazon rainforest to apartments and homes in New York, London, and Paris, millions of people derive great pleasure from keeping parrots as pets and cherished companions.

Few other types of pets are so adaptable as is the parrot, which makes easy adjustments to wide differences in housing, diet, weather, and social conditions. And, in the case of the larger parrot species that often live for 60 to 80 years if properly cared for, people might be fairly confident that they have a friend for life. Finally, after centuries of anecdotal reports and observations, new research has confirmed the positive psychological and physical health benefits that might result from caring for a companion parrot, as well as other types of affectionate, attentive, loving pets. A woman who owns both a Timneh African Grey and a Sun Conure, wrote that "my birds are very dear to me and after I got my birds they improved my health. They gave me a reason to keep going and not to give in to the pain in my back and legs. I am 67 years old, and I've found very good homes for them after I'm gone."

An Ancient Bond

A person who chooses to accept the enormous responsibility of caring for a parrot's housing, nutritional, hygienic, grooming, daily activity, and emotional/social needs, will find that such a companion enriches his or her life and home in many wonderful ways. The relationship between humans and parrots is an ancient one and we have made many terrible mistakes along the way, such as needlessly driving several psittacine species to extinction. In the United States, our own Carolina Parakeet was lost forever to "agricultural progress" in 1917.

More recently, worldwide habitat destruction has placed many species that we have always assumed to be "common" in great jeopardy. For instance, almost all the Mexican Redhead's breeding grounds in Mexico have been destroyed in favor of residential and commercial development. The small remaining parcels of natural habitat for this familiar parrot might easily fall victim, at this point, to any unforeseen natural disaster such as a tropical storm or industrial accident.

We humans have an obligation to protect our ancient and venerable

The Carolina Parakeet (Conurus carolinensis), the only parrot species indigenous to the United States, was lost forever in 1917.

relationship with the parrot, first, by working to support worldwide habitat conservation, breeding, and ornithological research efforts, and second, by providing the best possible care for the individual parrots that we welcome into our lives, hearts, and homes.

Chapter Two

A Parrot or Two, or Fifty, in Your Household

Social Animals

Parrots are, generally speaking, highly social animals that have a great need for physical and social contact with others. In the wild, of course, all this contact takes place between an individual parrot and members of its own flock—almost always within the same species. But the natural habitats of parrots, whether the dry grasslands of central Australia or the lush tropical rainforests of South America or Central Africa, are very special and increasingly rare places for our feathered companions to live. Most of us are unable to duplicate life in the rainforest within the confines or our living rooms or home aviaries.

Although we cannot truly duplicate in our lives the natural habitats of parrots, we can make these "short people in feathered pajamas," as one of the survey respondents fondly referred to members of order Psittaciformes, as comfortable and psychologically well adjusted as possible. In fact, as individuals who have assumed the responsibility of caring for a parrot's welfare, we are duty bound to do so.

In *The New Parrot Handbook* (1986; English translation of 1985 German book), Werner Lantermann provides an excellent list of considerations that any prospective parrot owner should contemplate *before* a parrot is brought into the home. Lantermann emphasizes that anyone thinking of acquiring a parrot must

A group of macaws in the wild socializing and preening each other.

be absolutely sure that proper care and nurturing of the companion parrot fits well with the person's lifestyle and temperament. Here are several items from his list of considerations.

Parrots are messy. They are not efficient eaters, and will drop at least as much as they eat. They are also picky eaters, and they will throw food around in search of that one extra-special morsel at the very bottom of the food dish. My Hahn's Macaw, Emmy Laura, only eats the red, yellow, and green morsels in the pelleted diet I feed her. For some reason, she hates the color purple, and she throws the purple pellets across the living room for fun. In fact, throwing food around is entertaining to most parrots, and if a parrot can make enough of a mess to get its human companion all excited, that's all the better.

Because parrots spend a considerable portion of each day grooming themselves (much as a cat does), they leave a trail of bits of old feathers and feather dust. Almost all manufacturers of cages for large hookbill parrots advertise that their products contain the mess so that your living room will stay clean; with the exception of cages that are fully enclosed in plexiglas, none of them really work. The problem is that if a parrot is left with most of each day to figure out how to outsmart the cage design and make a big mess anyway, you can bet that it'll do it! The bottom line is that you have to be willing to clean the food and water bowls

Careful cleaning of all food and water dishes is important for the routine health care of all parrots.

everyday with hot water and a disinfectant soap—rinse out the soapy water very well—every other day vacuum the area where your parrot lives, change the cage floor bedding daily (use newspaper to make this job much easier), and thoroughly wash, and again, rinse well, the entire cage and all its contents once every two months with an antibacterial disinfectant.

Parrots need access to fresh water all day, for two reasons: They need to drink it several times throughout the day, and most species of parrots also LOVE to bathe in it. All parrot owners should give their avian friends showers or baths regularly. My Blue and Gold Macaw, Zahava, the feminine form of the word "gold" in Hebrew, considers any mere "misting" with a spray bottle insufficient. She loves to get as wet as possible, and once a week I take her into the shower with me after I have rinsed off and lowered

the water temperature to lukewarm. It is important to remember that when a parrot's down feathers (the soft feathers close to their skin) get wet, they are unable to regulate their own body temperature very well and they can easily become chilled. So, you need to make sure your parrot stays warm until dry, and specifically, a parrot should not be left to dry off on its own if the ambient temperature is below 70°F (21°C). As for Zahava, she loves to occasionally be blow-dried after her shower with the blow-dryer set on "low" and held at least 15–24 inches (38–61 cm) from her.

As for drinking other liquids besides water, most parrots (not just fructivores, such as lories) will learn to enjoy fruit juices in moderation. Too much apple cider, orange juice, or grape juice isn't good for them, but fruits, and thus, their juices, should be a steady part of any parrot's diet. Oranges and orange juice are especially wonderful, being chock-full of calcium, phosphorus, iron, sodium, potassium, vitamin A, niacin, B-complex vitamins, traces of boron, and lots of vitamin C. In addition, if squeezed onto fresh foods that are left in food bowls for several hours at a time, especially in warmer climates, the mild acidity of orange juice helps to slow the growth of bacteria and other pathogens. Zahava and I share some juice each morning; she drinks five to six sips from my glass. It should be obvious that parrots have no business drinking coffee or other caffeinated beverages, or alcoholic beverages. Furthermore, any bird should be first quarantined (as described on page 55) before you decide to share a glass with or kiss your bird, in order to reduce the risk of bacterial or viral transmission from such beak-to-mouth contact. Moreover, transmission of fluids or food from mouth-to-beak should be avoided, as there is greater risk that your parrot may become infected by bacteria that is present in the human mouth and saliva.

Diets in Captivity

One reason many parrots have the potential to live much longer in captivity than we think they do in the wild is because they have a better chance of receiving a consistent nutritionally balanced diet, if they are fortunate enough to live with human friends who care enough to provide this. While it is perfectly reasonable to offer the occasional snack that has little nutritional value, such treats should be provided in moderation. For example, the favorite snack of a young Rainbow Lory from Portland, Maine, happens to be Cap' n Crunch Peanut Butter cereal. A White-eyed Conure from Spring Lake, Michigan, prefers cheese curls, and for his Orange Winged Amazon "sibling," it seems to be a tie between macaroni and cheese and buttered corn. Thankfully, there is an abundance of healthy choices of parrot food preparations that are tasty, smell great, (at least they do to us . . . not so much to the parrots who do not have strong sense of smell), and that provide a complete and balanced diet.

Seeds

Most parrots will pick one or two seed types that they prefer as their favorite food in the whole world, such as sunflower seeds or peanuts. If given the opportunity, a parrot will eat its favorite food to the exclusion of anything else. These special treats are usually very healthful in moderation, but not healthful if overconsumed. For instance, peanuts are a rich source of protein and several vitamins, in moderation, but contain too much fat to be eaten in excess. So, while it is a great idea to provide a few pieces of your parrots favorite food each day—perhaps as a reward for reinforcing good behaviors—you must be careful not to allow your parrot to develop any reluctance to eat a wide range of foods. A balanced diet for any self-respecting psittacine includes various seeds and grains (including a variety of seeds that you should allow to sprout for a few days in some wet paper towels, from time to time), fruit, berries, vegetables, and occasionally some animal protein in small

quantities, such as small amounts of water-packed tuna, hard-boiled egg, or cottage cheese. There are several books available that provide excellent discussions of proper diets for various types of parrots; these are listed in the Useful Addresses and Literature section on page 94. These issues will be discussed in greater detail in Chapter Six.

Protecting Your Parrot

Any parrot owner must ensure the safety of his or her feathered friend in the home and that means protecting the parrot from a number of different household dangers. Most parrots, with very few exceptions, will chew on just about anything that looks like

fun, including electrical wire, which could easily result in a fatal shock. Birds may also easily get caught and crushed in closing doors, can burn themselves on hot stoves, sustain concussions or broken necks from flying into large glass windows, or perish from toxic exposure to airborne pollutants, such as nicotine from cigarette smoke, or gases, such as harmful vapors released by heating Teflon-coated cookware above 530°F (250°C). Parrots can also catch colds or pneumonia as a result of a decreased immune response from constant exposure to drafts, and be poisoned by ingesting common objects that look like toys to them, such as household cleansers, ballpoint pen ink, alcohol, rust, plant fertilizers, and lead. Finally, while many house plants are perfectly safe

Harmful Plants

Common Name	Latin Name
Acokanthera	Acokanthera
Amaryllis	Amaryllis
Angel's Trumpet	Datura
Apricot	Prunus Armeniaca
Apple Tree	Malus
Avocado	Persea americana
Azalea	Rhododendron canadensis
Balsam Pear, Bitter Melon	Momordica charantia
Baneberry	Actaea rubra, A. pachyponda
Bird of Paradise	Poinciana and others
Bittersweet	Celastrus
Black Locust	Robinia pseudoacacia
Blue-green Algae	
Boxwood	Buxus spp
Buckhorn	Karwinskia humboltiana and related
Buttercup	Ranunculus
Caladium	Caladium
Calla Lily	Zantedeschia aethiopica
Castor Bean, Castor Oil	Ricinus communis
Cherry Tree	Prunus
Clematis	Clematic montana and related
Coral plant	Jatropha mutifida
Crocus, Autumn	Cholchicum autumnale
Cycad	Cycas revoluta
Daffodil	Narcissus tazetta
Daphne	Daphne mezerum
Delphinium	Delphinium
Devil's Ivory	Epipremnum aureum
Eggplant	Solanum melongena
Elderberry Tree	Sambucus mexicana
Elephant's Ears or Taro	Colocasia
European Pennyroyal	Mentha pulegium
Fig Tree	Ficus
Four O'Clock	Mirabilis jalapa
Foxglove	Digitalis purpurea
Heliotrope Leaves	Heliotropium
Henbane	Hyoscyamus niger

Harmful Plants continued

Common Name	Latin Name
Holly Leaves and Berries	*Ilex aquifolium* and related spp.
Horse Chestnut	*Aesculus hippocastanum* and related
Hyacinth	*Hyacinthus orientalis*
Hydrangea	*Hydrangea*
Iris	*Iris*
Ivy, Boston or English	*Hedera*
Jerusalem Cherry	*Solanum pseudocapsicum* and related
Jimsonweed	*Datura*
Juniper	*Juniperus*
Larkspur	*Delphinium*
Laurel	*Kalmia*
Lily of the Valley	*Convalleria majalis*
Marijuana	*Cannabis sativa*
Milkweed	*Asclepias*
Mistletoe	*Phoradendron villosum*
Mock Orange	*Philadelphus*
Monkshood	*Aconitum*
Morning Glory Seeds	*Ipomoea violacea*
Mushrooms	*Amanita* and many others
Narcissus	*Narcissus*
Oak	*Quercus*
Oleander	*Nerium oleander*
Peach Tree	*Prunus persica*
Pear Tree and Seeds	*Pyrus*
Peony	*Paeonia officinalis*
Periwinkle	*Vinca minor, V. rosea*
Peyote	*Lophophora williamsii*
Philodendron	*Philodendron*
Pigweed	*Amaranthus*
Plum Tree	*Prunus*
Poison Hemlock	*Conium maculatum*
Poison Ivy and Poison Oak	*Toxicodendron*
Poison Sumac	*Rhux vernix*
Poinsettia	*Euphobia pulcherrima*
Poppy	*Papever somniferum* and related
Potato, Plants and Tubers	*Solanum tuberosum*

Harmful Plants continued

Common Name	Latin Name
Primrose	*Primula*
Privet	*Ligustrum vulgare*
Ragwort	*Senecio jacobea* and related
Red Maple	*Acer rubrum*
Rhododendron	*Rhododendron*
Rhubarb Leaves	*Rheum rhubarbarum*
Rosary Pea	*Abrus precatorius*
Sage	*Salvia officinalis*
Shamrock Plant	*Medicago lupulina, Trilofium repens, Oxalis acetosella*
Skunk Cabbage	*Symplocarpus foetidus*
Snowdrop	*Golanthus nivalis*
Sorrel	*Rumex; Oxalis*
Spurges	*Euphorbia*
Star of Bethlehem	*Ornithogalum umbellatum*
Sweet Pea	*Lathyrus odoratus*
Tobacco	*Nicotiana*
Tomato Stems and Leaves	*Lycopersicon esculentum*
Tulip	*Tulipa*
Virginia Creeper	*Panthenocisus quinquefolia*
Vetches	*Vicia*
Water Hemlock	*Cicuta*
Waxberry	*Symphoricarpos albus*
Wisteria	*Wisteria*
Yam Bean	*Pachyrhizus erosus*
Yew, all types	*Taxus*

for your parrot to munch on, there are a wide range of plants that are toxic to birds if eaten.

Starting on page 17 is a partial list of common houseplants and trees, parts of which are poisonous, such as the bulb, leaves, stem, bark, or roots. Parrots should not have access to them. Some Latin names refer to the harmful species or subspecies of the plants.

This list of potentially harmful plants is not exhaustive, and because plant names often vary by region and by reference guide, you should consult your local nursery or your veterinarian to check the names of the plants in your home.

On the other hand, there are plenty of common houseplants that are perfectly safe for your companion parrot to nibble on, such as roses,

Nontoxic Trees and Vines

Common Name	Latin Name
Ailanthus	*Ailanthus altissima*
Ash	*Fraxinus* spp.
Aspen	*Populus* spp.
Bamboo	
Beech, American and European	*Fagus, Nothofagus*
Birch	*Betula* spp.
Chicory	*Cichorium intybus*
Coffee	*Coffea arabica*
Dogwood	*Cornus* spp.
Elm	*Ulmus* spp.
Fir, including Balsam, Douglas, Subalpine, and White	*Abies* spp.
Eucalyptus	*Eucalyptus* sp.
Magnolia	*Magnolia spp.*
Manzanita	*Arctostapylos manzanita*
Pine, Ponderosa, Virginia, and white	*Pinus, ponderosa, virginiensis, et strobus*
Raspberry	*Rubus strigosus*
Spruce	*Picea* spp.
Smooth, Shiny, and Staghorn Sumac	*Rhus copallina, glabra,* and *typhina* spp.
Thistle	*Cirsium* spp.
Willow	*Salix* spp.

African violets, aloe, chamomile, begonias, garlic, parsley, peppermint, dill, jade plants, spider plants, lilacs, petunias, and marigolds.

In fact, most fruit trees and vines, such as blueberry, grape, and bayberry, are perfectly safe and your parrot will have a great time and benefit from excellent exercise if supplied often with branches with the bark left on. For example, although poison sumac *(Rhux vernix)* is dangerous for birds, other types of sumac such as the smooth, shiny, and staghorn subspecies (see page 20) are very well suited as perching branches for both small and medium-size parrots. Trees that are safe and potentially nutritionally beneficial to use as perches in cages are listed on page 20.

Choosing Life with a Parrot

Noise

Another important topic to consider, before deciding to spend the next several decades of your life with a parrot, is that, with a few exceptions, most species of parrots are noisy. That is, most parrots are normally very noisy if they are healthy and happy, and it is both typical and expected of them that they screech loudly several times each day, especially early in the morning and at dusk. You need to carefully consider whether you, your family, and your neighbors (especially if you live in an apartment or townhouse with shared walls) are not just willing, but eager to put up with these daily "jungle sounds." Unfortunately, many parrot owners have had to give their pets up for adoption because of complaints from neighbors or other family members.

Babies and Small Children

It is important to understand that large parrots can pose a danger to babies and small children. When a new baby joins the family, your parrot, which is used to being the center of attention, may become jealous and act aggressively toward your child if allowed the opportunity to do so. Rather than giving up your bird, expect a period of adjustment during which your parrot will require extra-close supervision. *Under no circumstances should you leave a baby or very young child alone in a room with an uncaged parrot.* The greatest risk to a young child is from a parrot inflicting painful wounds— scratches or bites—because the child is unable to anticipate the sudden jabs of a parrot's beak. School-aged children usually have no problem with learning to get along with an uncaged parrot, as they quickly get to know the bird's habits and read its moods.

Daily Care

Unlike your cat, which you can leave for a couple of days with an extra supply of food and water and a clean litterbox, your parrot

A New Life

This was the sad story of one 25-year-old Amazon Parrot that was finally adopted into a good home in Cortland, New York. His new owner wrote, "We acquired our Amazon two months ago as an abuse case. He was in ill health, vicious, and in a tiny rusted cage that he had never been out of in almost 25 years. He was wild-caught. He had never had a toy or been handled, and he didn't know what fresh fruit and vegetables were. He is happy and healthy, loves his fruit and veggies, glee-fully plays with his toys, has a huge cage, and comes out to explore around the house daily. He lets me handle him, massage him, and play with him, but he allows no one else near him. Although the rest of my family has consistently tried to win his trust and affection, he will do nothing but fiercely bite them. He has never bitten me—even from the first touch. We are hoping in time that he will learn to trust other members of my family."

requires daily care. Because parrots are such messy, inefficient eaters, they don't save food for the next day very well, and they need a fresh supply of food and water usually twice a day. On weekdays, I typically feed Zahava every morning before leaving for work, and again at around 6:00 P.M. I'll admit, on the weekends I spoil her rotten with special treats and toys. Parrots also differ greatly from cats in that they are highly social animals that crave contact with members of their flock (this means you). This is especially true of parrots that are raised singly as pets. In this case, you are their family, and they need daily reassurance from you or some other human who can fill in for a few days, that all is well in the jungle. In other words, you must plan ahead for how your parrot will be taken care of if you leave town on vacation, even if it is just for one day. Some avian veterinarians and pet stores board birds for a fee, but no matter where you board your bird, visit first. How clean are the cages? Are the food and water dishes cleaned and refilled regularly enough?

Pet Sitters

Many people, including me, prefer to rely on the services of an experienced pet sitter. Pet sitting is a rapidly growing cottage industry and such a service probably is available in your community. Check the pet sitter's references and ask important questions:

- How much experience does the pet sitter have in caring for parrots?
- Does the pet sitter know how to handle home emergencies, such

as stopping bleeding if a blood feather is broken?
- Is the pet sitter aware of the common warning signs of serious illness, such as sitting listlessly in the cage with puffed-up plumage, diarrhea, or watery eyes?

And remember to always leave the name and telephone number of your trusted avian veterinarian with your pet sitter in case of an emergency.

Many parrot owners will go to impressive extremes in order not to leave their companion bird unoccupied. One lucky seven-year-old male Umbrella Cockatoo named Baby that lives in Maryland rides with his parents cross-country. The cockatoo, toy poodle, and two human adults all drive in a commercial truck together on a full-time basis. Says the owner, "He gets a lot of atten-

tion. Baby rides on the back of my seat during the day, and he rides in bed with me at night. Besides our attention, he entertains in truck stops, weigh stations, shippers' places, consignees' places, and at our different agents' office. If he hears a strange voice he immediately begins talking and showing off."

The responsibility a parrot owner assumes for the proper care and nurturing of the bird is huge, and it won't lessen over time. Depending on the species of parrot you choose for a companion, especially the larger hookbills, it is likely that your parrot will live longer than you do. Anyone who has raised a child knows full well and shudders at the mention of the "terrible twos." You need to understand, preferably before you make any investment in a

They Never Grow Up

Valerie, an owner of a cockatoo in El Cajon, California, aptly stated that parrots are "clever little people with feather pajamas on. My only struggle with my parrot is to try to understand the messages he sends me. The rewards and companionship are great!"

parrot, that they are just as inquisitive, creative, playful, affection-starved, and temperamental as most two-year-old human children—but your parrot probably will never act like an adult.

Too many people purchase parrots when they are small, cute, and relatively quiet; and they are ill-prepared to make the necessary adjustments in their own lives to raise a healthy, well-adjusted adolescent and adult parrot in the coming years. When parrots get older and start to reach sexual maturity, and they become more temperamental, territorial, and "nippy" with people of whom they are not fond, the all-too-often response is to lock them up in a cage—that is, prison—in "solitary confinement" for the rest of their lives.

The parrot is an intelligent, perceptive, and highly social animal. These behavioral and cognitive talents make it well suited to a life in the forest canopy or open grasslands. In our homes, however, parrots are entirely dependent on us to supply all that they require to be safe, well nourished, healthy, and stimulated physically, intellectually, and emotionally.

Chapter Three

Sex and the Single Parrot

Most people who are interested in owning a parrot as a pet do not start out with the intention of building an indoor-outdoor aviary and amassing the knowledge and experience necessary to successfully breed birds. Rather, these interests in aviculture develop in time, and they are more or less involuntary if you are not careful. I'll never forget going to pick out my first bird in 1986, a baby cockatiel, from a breeder in Michigan. My girlfriend and I walked into the front door of his house in a nice residential neighborhood and were shocked to find that his avicultural interests had overtaken every square foot of his home. As he greeted us at the front door, a baby Blue and Gold Macaw waddled after him searching for food, and the house looked as if hundreds of parrots had trimmed their beaks by chewing up all of the interior moldings, railings, banisters, stairs, and some of the dry wall. We were not at all surprised to learn that his wife had recently left him and that his neighbors were complaining.

Your Parrot's True Nature

At any rate, most of us initially purchase a young bird that is sexually immature, or an older bird that is at first unsure of its new surroundings or daily routine. In both cases, when your bird first comes

The bond between parrot and human can be very strong.

25

home with you, the chances are that it will be quiet, docile, non-demanding, certainly a bit frightened, and not generally aggressive or "nippy" in its play. You might think to yourself, "What a sweet temperament my parrot has!" But just wait...you ain't seen nothin' yet! When any parrot that is housed alone and does not come with a chosen mate moves into a new home, these behaviors are common, and the individual animal's "true colors" are not likely to emerge for at least several weeks. Why? It depends on the bird.

Parrots Love Routine

All parrots, young or old, thrive on daily routines. They wake up around the same time every morning, they learn to expect the same amount of playtime with their family each day, and they like to go to bed at the same time every night. When you bring your parrot home for the first time, this routine hasn't been set yet but over the first few weeks, these daily rituals become the general rules of the household. Your parrot will become accustomed to this daily routine and will become upset if this routine is abruptly changed and any new rules are not adhered to. Of course, most parrots will adjust if their favored flockmate must leave to go to work during the day. A Congo African Grey from

Kansas City, named Seuss, bids her owner good-bye when she leaves for work in the morning by saying, "Go work, buy bird food." Another Congo African Grey from Pennsylvania really loves breakfast each morning, and will tell his owner, "Papa, I want waffle breakfast."

The Importance of Companionship

There are other reasons, besides the lack of an established daily routine, that parrots new to their households might show different temperaments at first than they will eventually demonstrate. It takes time for the new arrival to adjust to its surroundings. A parrot that has been abruptly removed from its familiar environment, whether among the trees of a tropical forest or in the cozy living room of a former owner, will take a while to bond to a new human or avian flockmate. In the case of sexually mature parrots (macaws, for instance, don't really reach full sexual maturity until about four years old), they may be lonely for a flockmate that has died or moved away. To my knowledge, all parrots pair-bond to at least some extent, whether to another parrot or to a human substitute. Parrots are highly social animals that enjoy living in large groups (flocks) as well as bonding closely to one other parrot. Any parrot that is not permitted to form a close emotional bond with another individual, human or parrot, is in great danger of developing severe and permanent psychological problems, weight loss and malnutrition, difficult-to-control feather plucking behavior, and probably a decreased immune response, and therefore an increased susceptibility to opportunistic infections. Parrots raised in isolation from anything resembling a mate almost always develop severe behavioral disturbances and have shortened life expectancies. Although much research still needs to be done in this area, it is quite possible that these unfortunate animals might also be prone to a decreased immune response to opportunistic infections as a result of the impact of psychological illness on normal brain function.

Pair-Bonding

Any older parrot brought into a new family needs to develop a new pair-bond relationship. At first, it typically will not favor one member of the household to the exclusion of others; however, although some species of parrots are more likely than others to form close and affectionate bonds with multiple family members to at least some extent (in my experience, Jardine's Parrots, certain species of "miniature" macaws, and many species of cockatoos are often, but certainly not always, more permissive in this regard), other species such as

African Greys and most Amazon Parrots will quickly select their favorite human in the flock to preferentially bond with. In these cases, it is extremely important to apply various behavioral techniques to teach these animals to enjoy their time with other members of the flock in addition to their bonded mate. This isn't always easy, but there are some sources of excellent advice including a recent book by Mattie Sue Athan (see Useful Addresses and Literature page 94).

These observations usually hold true for young birds that are being introduced to their first home. Healthy baby parrots are "love sponges," and most cockatoo owners would agree that these Australasian species never grow out of this. But most babies do grow up, and, although if raised properly, never stop being wonderful and affectionate pets, they will nonetheless begin to assert themselves in their households more intently. It is at this early stage that proper behavioral training is most important, and it is your responsibility to use humane, nonthreatening methods to teach your pet that you, and not your bird, are the dominant member of your flock. These issues will be discussed more later.

Most of us who jump into the avicultural world for the first time bring home a single, young, sweet parrot that we hope will bond to us as its flockmate. Typically, but not always, the person in the home who provides most of the warmth, security,

Merlin's Jealousy

For an example of jealousy just ask the owner of Merlin, a Red Lored Amazon, in Rochester, New York. She wrote that, without question, Merlin sees her as his mate and he often proves this to her by depositing regurgitated food into her ears. Merlin seems to be intensely jealous of her husband and once, when the hapless spouse walked by, Merlin lunged forward and his right talon broke off. After a cast was placed on Merlin's foot and leg, setting the foot in the open position so Merlin could perch, he quickly learned that he could fly past the husband and whack him in the head with his hard cast by "moving his foot sideways on a close fly-by!"

Merlin also has other strong likes and dislikes at home. For instance, he loves anything that is colored red, and he "reacts violently" to anything colored brown or black, such as raisins. As funny as this sounds, it isn't at all uncommon. Individual parrots have very distinct preferences, and many birds will prefer to play with one sex (of humans) over another, or people with or without beards and mustaches, or other distinguishing physical characteristics. Two Timneh African Greys who were hand-raised by Tracy, a woman of Asian descent who lives in Hacienda Heights, California, clearly prefer to be approached by other Asians, and "they become agitated by most non-Asians who invade their space, until the birds get to know them." These Timnehs apparently have "never become agitated by Asians on the first meeting, and they have become attracted to Asian females on the first meeting." The parrots seem to think of Tracy's husband, a Caucasian male, as the "bad guy . . . unless, of course, I am unavailable for a few days." Tracy reports.

feather preening, and meals will become the lucky chosen human to whom your bird bonds. Even if all these duties are split equally between two people, it is an instinctual behavior for the parrot to at least slightly favor one person over another in order to select a mate. Again, reasonably effective behavioral techniques can be used to keep this urge from being expressed too strongly, but most parrots exhibit a clear desire to bond with one special person to at least some degree. When this happens, there's plenty of room for jealousies to develop. If you are selected by your parrot as its mate, then your human companion may become an object of jealousy; that is, your parrot may decide that it needs to actively compete with your companion for your attention.

It is important to learn what your companion parrot's specific preferences are, both for the safety of others, if, for instance, your parrot routinely nips or lunges at males who try to pick it up, and in order to design a daily routine and environment in which your bird will be happy and interested each day. Of course, some strong preferences need to be modified with proper behavioral interventions. For instance, with few exceptions, your parrot must have a healthy diet with a variety of foods. If, for example, your parrot develops a predilection for peanuts to the exclusion of any other type of food offered, such a strong preference must be corrected quickly.

Sexual Maturation and Behavioral Change

A parrot's behavior undergoes certain changes as it progresses through sexual maturity and reaches breeding age. Specifically, mature male parrots—and to a lesser extent female parrots—exhibit hormonally induced sexual behaviors during the breeding season. During these times that typically occur once or twice a year, your normally affectionate and docile bird may become more aggressive, loud, and unpredictable in its behavior. It is important for you to learn to recognize these times, which may last from a few weeks to a few months, and to adjust your own expectations and reactions accordingly. It is espe-

cially during these cycles that you do not want your mature parrot to feel dominant over you, for instance, by being allowed to stay on your shoulder above eye level; if it becomes aggressive, leave it alone. A normally sweet parrot may easily lose control in the midst of a hormonal surge and sexual frenzy, and bite hard at your face or eyes. Remember that these are natural, temporary phases that all healthy adult parrots go through each year, and your parrot will not grow out of this until it is very old.

Parrot Societies and Your Living Room

Because parrots are extremely social animals they thrive on close contact with their larger flocks as well as with one other special mate with whom they have pair-bonded. As such, all parrots enjoy being integral members of your household, and although they, just like us, need their quiet "I-need-to-be-alone-now" time, including about 10 to 12 hours of restful sleep each night, they thrive on being in the middle of all of the noise and activity in the home. For this reason, it is a terrible idea to relegate your parrot, especially if it is housed singly, to a room in the house where there is little foot traffic from other family members, and where the bird cannot hear and observe what's going on.

Screaming

When your parrot screams on occasion, it is often doing so to make contact with other family members that it cannot see. In the wild, members of flocks call to each other constantly to provide continual reassurance that they are near and that all is well. It is very distressing for your companion parrot to be able to hear you in another room but to not be able to see you. Its normal reaction is to call to you to make sure you are near. If you, in turn, scream back at the parrot, you are actually reinforcing this behavior; your screaming back is precisely what your bird wants you to do. If this is a behavior that you don't particularly care for—and most of us do not—then there are two things you can do:

1. Remember that all healthy parrots scream once or twice a day; if they did not, this would be a warning sign that something might be very wrong with your pet;
2. Be aware that if you always get angry and scream back, you are actually reinforcing the parrot's desire to scream in the first place.

The best response is to call back softly to your bird, and let it see that you are nearby.

Communal Living

Some parrot owners have been known to get a bit carried away by communal living. A woman writing on behalf of her husband, two Congo African Greys, and a Goffin's Cockatoo, noted that "We all live in close proximity. During the day when my husband and I are out, the birds have their own room and cages, otherwise, when we are home we have separate perches in the living room plus separate perches in the bedroom for sleeping and roosting. We also shower together with a special shower perch for the birds. My husband and I perch on the couch and sleep on a bed."

Some owners find that sometimes they have to sneak around the house to avoid letting their parrots know they are home. One woman wrote that she was out late one night, and was unable to spend the usual "quality time" with her two-year-old Rainbow Lory that evening. When she came home, "all was dark and quiet as I crept past the bird cages, when suddenly I heard my Lory, Iris, say in a very accusing tone, 'Where were you?'"

Breeding for Survival

It is important to stress that it has become increasingly important for both professional and amateur aviculturists to be involved in the captive breeding of species that are endangered in the wild. Over the past few decades there has been much success in breeding birds whose numbers in the wild have been seriously declining. The establishment of breeding groups, and a large enough population of captive animals to ensure the health of the overall gene pool, has become vital to maintaining species that otherwise would have very bleak futures. As of 1992, approximately 84 percent of all parrot species known to aviculture have been successfully bred in captivity; that percentage has been rising each year as more information about various species' special needs for breeding are becoming known. Still, amateur aviculturists are in a position to contribute to the survival of many endangered species, a potential that has yet to be fully realized.

It is beyond the scope of this book to present the critical information necessary to both successfully and responsibly breed parrots. Anyone interested in this challenging and rewarding area of aviculture has much to learn about the provision of proper species-specific nesting sites and materials, parent and hatchling dietary needs, incubation, hatching, early postnatal care, and sexing techniques, as well as at least a basic understanding of genetics and the protection of genetic diversity within any given species. Fortunately, there are several excellent resources available for those who have these interests, and although I have listed several written sources (see Useful Addresses and Literature page 94), no book will provide as much information as you will receive from spending time "training" under an experienced breeder. In addition, there are community parrot enthusiast bird clubs located throughout North America and Europe; members of these clubs, who are breeders as well, often enjoy teaching others who are sincerely interested. Many of these clubs also offer classes to teach members about the basics of responsible psittacine breeding.

Chapter Four

Parrots and Four-Legged Companions

Here's the family recipe for the microwave casserole I occasionally make for my psittacines and canine. Please note that, although all the ingredients in this recipe are of great nutritional benefit for most parrots, this dish is saved as a treat the birds get about once every six weeks. Cheese should be fed to a parrot only in moderation and in small amounts, as it contains some lactose, a milk sugar, although most of this is left behind in the whey during the manufacturing process. In the wild, birds normally would not ingest dairy products, and as a result they do not produce the necessary enzyme, *lactase*, to digest the lactose sugar. If birds do consume too much lactose, they will develop diarrhea and, most likely, plenty of discomfort—not unlike people who live with lactose intolerance. In small quantities cheese is a good source of several vitamins and protein.

Sharing Food and Company

Although my dog is more than happy to share some of my parrot's food, the reverse is not true. It is not appropriate to feed your parrot dog food, dry or canned. When I first adopted Zahava, she had been fed only dog food and poor-quality sunflower seeds—the kind that you buy at hardware stores for outdoor bird feeders—for the first two years of her life. As a result, she was terribly undernourished and listless, and she suffered from an intestinal parasitic

Dogs and parrots often form bonds, but should be supervised when together.

Zavi and Buddha's Egg Casserole Surprise

Ingredients:
1 large egg, scrambled, with shell included
   (chop shell very well with a fork into tiny pieces)
2 tsp. cooked whole-grain rice
1 Tbs. raisins
½ tsp. ground, unsalted peanuts
1 dash nutmeg
1 dash cinnamon
1 tsp. grated Romano cheese

Directions:
Mix all ingredients together and spoon mixture into a small, shallow, microwave oven-safe container, such as a soup bowl. Cover with plastic wrap and cook on high setting for approximately two minutes until egg is cooked thoroughly. Let cool 10 minutes, and make sure there are no hot spots in the food that might burn the parrot's crop.

Serving Instructions:
Half of the casserole goes to the dog, and is devoured within microseconds. The other half should be divided into about five servings for a single parrot; the remainder may be kept covered in the refrigerator for up to two days.

infection that probably had been transmitted from one of several other parrots confined under similar conditions in her previous home.

Sometimes, a parrot will search for its canine friend in order to have some fun. When bored, one particular 1½-year-old Congo African Grey will call for "her" dog by saying "Mai Ling, Mai Ling...where's that damn dog!" Indeed, parrots and dogs learn to get along in the house surprisingly well. When we are at work each day I am convinced that my dog and parrot rely on each other for company. It is, in fact, not uncommon for

parrots and dogs to become great friends. For example, Simon, a 1½-year-old Double Yellowhead Amazon, lives in Little Rock, Arkansas, with an Australian Shepherd named Bonnie. Bonnie is evidently terrified of thunderstorms, and during such storms, Simon is quick to assure her: "It's okay, Bonnie." He then sings to the dog and climbs down from his perch to preen her.

Still, not all dogs and parrots become close friends, and you need to introduce your pets to each other slowly and with great care. As friendly as my dog and parrot are to

My Puppy and My Parrot

Approximately four months after adopting, at age two, our Blue and Gold Macaw, Zahava, who, like many birds, was rescued from a physically and emotionally abusive home environment, and three months after moving into our first house, my girlfriend and I adopted a puppy from the local dog shelter. When I found Buddha, a 75-pound, 15-month-old Rottweiler at the shelter, he had been on death row for eight days. I stopped at a pay phone on the way home from the shelter, and left a message that I was coming home with a puppy. When I arrived home, my girlfriend expected me to get out of the car holding a cute, little furball. When she saw Buddha walk in the house, she was stunned.

Buddha is now very much a part of my nuclear family, and he is well-trained, obedient, gentle, and friendly. He is also submissive to, and slightly afraid of, our two-pound Blue and Gold Macaw. Essentially, Zahava claimed ownership of the house first and she has set the ground rules for the household. On occasion she'll climb off her jungle gym and waddle around the floor to search for humans throughout the house; Buddha keeps his distance or he risks a nip on his nose by her large, black beak. When he gets too playful and rowdy around her, she'll let him know by saying "No, Buddha, no!"

Of course, they do have their tender moments when she'll tug gently on his large jowls, or when he'll patiently wait under her perch while she drops pieces of food to watch him eat. Among my Rottweiler's favorite foods are LaFeber's Nutriberries (a nutritionally complete parrot food), vegetables that she drops for him, and an occasional egg casserole with cheese, rice, and raisins that I make for them.

each other I would never leave them in a room together unsupervised, with my parrot outside her cage. I know of a Rottweiler that lives with a nine-year-old male White-Fronted Amazon named Buffet in Daytona Beach, Florida. According to their owner they usually get along quite well, but one day she mistakenly left them unsupervised, and when she walked into the house, she heard the Amazon screaming from inside a trash can, "Don't bite me! Don't bite me!" The dog was sniffing around the can, but couldn't get to the bird. When his owner pulled the bird out of the trash, it exclaimed "Oh, boy!"

Kittens and Parrots

If kittens are raised with your parrots, they may also form very comfortable relationships with birds. Of course, for some cats the predatory instinct is more irrepressible than for others, and you need to pay close attention to the possibility that your cat's hunting instinct may be just a bit too strong to warrant leaving your 3-ounce budgie alone on an open perch near him. In her excellent book on parrot behavioral training, Mattie Sue Athan recommends that for particularly predatory cats, the smallest bird that can safely be introduced into the home may be the Monk Parakeet (also called a Quaker Parakeet), which weighs about 5 ounces. Without question, you will have the most success in mixing feline and avian pets in your home if you raise your kitten from an early age with your bird.

An important point to remember: Most cats carry bacteria, *pasteurella,* in their saliva; if transmitted to your parrot, it may result in a fatal bacterial infection. Cats and birds, therefore should never share the same food and water bowls, and it is wise to keep your kitties' claws clipped regularly to prevent scratches. If your parrot is ever scratched by your cat, the bird requires immediate antibiotic therapy.

Of course, not all parrots and cats in the same household form harmonious friendships, and sometimes one becomes noticeably jealous of the attention the other is receiving from their mutually favorite human. One five-year-old Congo African Grey that I know of tells the resident feline in the household, "go away

Grey-Grey the Trainer

An African Grey, named Grey-Grey, who lives in New Britain, Connecticut, is practicing to be a dog obedience trainer. When the dog, an English Setter named Q.E., is allowed in a room with Grey-Grey, he will shout, "Q.E., come!" but the dog will ignore him. Grey-Grey will then get a food pellet and drop it on the floor. Of course, the dog will come over to eat the pellet, and Grey-Grey will say, "Q.E . . . no, no, no, go lie down!" When the dog happens to lie down of his own accord, the parrot will say, "Good Q.E.! Good dog!"

cat!" whenever the cat tries to move onto her owner's lap.

Note: There are some four-legged species of pets, such as ferrets, that never mix well with parrots, under any circumstances. Ferrets have been known to attack and fatally wound even the largest of hookbill parrots when given half a chance.

Introducing the Animals

If you contemplate adding yet another class within the animal kingdom to your household, it is best to introduce your mature parrot to the new cat or dog when they are young. A puppy or kitten will adapt best. Bring them together initially for

Parrots and Cats

Sometimes parrots and cats can form unusually close relationships. An 18-year-old Moluccan Cockatoo named Robinson Caruso, from Portland, Oregon, has just such a relationship with one of the cats he lives with. He has befriended a household cat named Katrina. Apparently, Katrina suffers from epilepsy, and the cockatoo alerts his owner with an "alarm call" just before the cat has seizures. This alarm is often signaled at times when the two animals cannot even see each other. The phenomenon of an animal somehow sensing when another animal or a human is about to have a seizure, perhaps by detecting minute electrical changes in the brain preceding the onset of a full seizure, has been reported anecdotally countless numbers of times. Another cat in the same household "has a special 'meow' that she uses only to communicate with the cockatoo." This meow usually leads to the cockatoo launching into his "macho and loud rendition" of "I'm a great and wonderful bird and King of the Empire!"

Arlo, a 19-year-old Congo African Grey from California, has always lived with cats, and prefers to "hang out" with his current feline friend, Penny, when given the chance. Arlo will wander around the house to look for Penny, and he will perch near her in order to sneak in a "playful nip now and then." Arlo's owner knows that he is the dominant animal in this relationship, perhaps because his owner explained to Penny "how she must protect Arlo and not harm him. Sometimes, though, he pushes her too far" and gets a scratch.

short periods of time, and always under close supervision. Any attempt to raise parrots in close proximity to other pets, including animals that are much larger than parrots, presents a set of unusual challenges. Under the best of conditions, a parrot's behavior is, at times, unpredictable. The same holds true for cats and, although to a lesser degree, for dogs. As a result, raising different pets together in the same home always carries a certain amount of risk of harm to one or both animals, and *under no circumstances should a parrot and another pet ever be left alone unsupervised.* If you manage the process slowly and carefully, however, your parrot and its four-legged companion will often develop what appears to be a lasting friendship. Just this morning I watched Zahava climb off her jungle gym to chase my Rottweiler around the house after a rawhide bone they both like to play with.

Chapter Five

A Parrot's Cage Is Its Castle

Most of us do not have the physical space, financial resources, or needed time to build an aviary as a new addition to our homes. Also, unless you live in a warm, southern climate, it is difficult to design and build a freestanding indoor-outdoor aviary that is appropriate for use throughout the year. Most of us rely on one or more cages to house our feathered companions; thus, the question arises as to what location in the home is the ideal place to put the cage.

Where to Put the Cage

Some people elect to set aside one room of the house as the "bird room." I think that is an especially poor choice for families that own a single parrot but if you own several parrots, they can be placed in adjacent cages with the hope that they might entertain each other throughout the day. Parrots may be kept in fairly close proximity to each other,

once each parrot has been quarantined in a separate room for 90 days in order to reduce the risk of spreading transmittable viral infections from one animal to another. Even in this situation, however, one has to wonder why a family would keep parrots that are housed in a private room and away from the daily commotion and activity of the family.

Unfortunately, after the novelty of owning an exotic bird has worn off, as is bound to happen, there often is a tendency to treat the parrot like home exercise equipment. When many people first buy a treadmill, for instance, it is frequently and eagerly used. Unless one is truly devoted to daily exercise, however, over time there is a tendency to slowly slack off and let the relatively new and expensive treadmill collect dust. One of the reasons for this is the perception that the use of the equipment is just a bit inconvenient. A remedy for this is to place the treadmill in a location in the house where it is seen often, so that its owner is often reminded that it is easy to step on and use it.

There is also the potential for the perception of relative inconvenience to develop with anything we own—including our pets—if they are relegated to a part of the house that is not used frequently for other purposes. Sadly, many people initially choose to purchase a parrot because it is a unique pet to own, and it is thus regarded as something of a status symbol. When the novelty of such purchases wears off after awhile, these owners are left with an intelligent, highly social animal that needs to feel that it is part of the flock, that is, the family. The way to prevent raising an unhappy, poorly socialized parrot is to place the cage in a highly trafficked area of the household, such as the family room where individuals relax when home.

It is a good idea to place the cage with one side against a wall of the room, as this provides an extra sense of security for your bird. Remember that in the wild, parrots are prey animals that are always vigilant about watching their backs. In addition, it is not a good idea to place the cage in the kitchen, as the parrot would be exposed to numerous fumes and rapid temperature changes, all of which are potentially harmful to the parrot's sensitive respiratory system. Finally, when choosing where to place the cage within your home, remember that parrots do not have sweat glands and they can easily overheat if the cage is placed where it will receive a lot of direct sunlight,

unless the bird also has the opportunity to retreat to shade. Although many species of psittacines are from the hot tropics, they are used to spending most of their time in at least partial shade and, depending on the particular species, often at high elevations. In the wild, from the tropical lowlands of Brazil to the arid grasslands of Australia, parrots are able to rely on a variety of strategies to cool themselves; most of these opportunities are lost if your bird is confined to a cage, during the heat of the summer, in your own backyard.

Caging Your Birds Together

Some parrot owners who keep more than one bird choose to house their pets together, with two or more parrots in the same cage, and again, proper cage size is extremely important. In this situation, there is the possibility that your pets will bond more closely to each other than to you. For some owners, this pattern of socialization and pair-bonding is either desired, especially in situations where human members of the flock are away from home very often, or at least seen as acceptable, whereas for others the feeling of being the "third wheel" in the flock can be very disheartening. One owner of both a five-year-old Blue-Fronted Amazon and a five-year-old Double Yellow Head Amazon wrote that each parrot has its own large cage placed "about a foot apart in the family room off the kitchen," She picked that part of the house because "they have a nice view of the birds in the yard through the patio doors." Her parrots are kept caged while she is at work and are taken out for playtime separately during the week. On weekends, however, she pushes the two cages together to let them play. She wrote that "we are a strange threesome, and alliances within our triad are always changing. I used to let the two Amazons spend more time together, until they started to leave me out of the family."

Temperature and Humidity

Those of us who live in northern climates are thrilled when the warmer spring and summer weather draws near. We can open our windows to allow fresh air in, bathe our birds without worrying that they'll become chilled, and rely less on artificial lighting to prolong the shorter daylight hours of the winter months. This is also the time of year when we turn on our air conditioners. Conversely, I have friends who live in south Florida who rarely ever turn off their air conditioning. Is air conditioning harmful to birds? Generally, the answer to this question is no. As long as the cage is not placed directly in front of the air conditioning vent, which would constantly blow cold air directly into the cage,

and the temperature is maintained at a consistent level that is not too cold (that is, below 65°F [18°C]), the use of air conditioning may prove to be beneficial in that the decreased humidity will slow the growth of molds and mildew.

In addition, with a more constant temperature and humidity, soft foods such as fruits and vegetables stay fresh longer. Nonetheless, it is always important to remove such foods a few hours after they are placed in the food dish, to discourage the growth of molds, bacteria, and the attraction of unwanted insects, although a little insect protein in its diet will not hurt your bird.

This rule is especially important for birds in outdoor enclosures in warm, humid climates. Well-known parrot behavior expert, Susan Chamberlain, recommends that in subtropical climates it is "necessary

A variety of fresh fruits and vegetables should be offered each day, but they should be removed after a few hours, before they begin to spoil.

hulls, food pellet leftovers, mashed grapes, banana mush, feathers, and dust is of paramount importance; for others, the decision is primarily made based on factors such as ease of access to food and water dishes, color, construction materials, or other decorating concerns.

No matter how you arrive at your decision to purchase one cage style over another, there are several important issues that need to be considered:

- **Confinement.** It is entirely unfair to confine a parrot permanently to any cage. The cage is important as a place of refuge and security, and your bird will automatically view the cage as a safe place to eat and sleep; however, all birds need plenty of exercise, and they should have an open perch or jungle gym to play on when you are at home. By the way, *don't even think about using a chain to shackle your parrot to a stand.* There is no need for this whatsoever, and not only does such a practice eliminate the possibility of healthy exercise, but the bird can become severely injured if it is frightened or accidentally slips off the perch.

- **Size.** Most first-time parrot owners tend to make the mistake of purchasing a cage that is too small. If the interior dimensions of the cage are too small to allow the parrot to stretch its wings completely and move about without trouble, the poor animal is condemned to a life of physical

to remove uneaten portions of fresh food from outdoor cages after about three hours during the warm, humid months." Under such conditions, I would recommend removing fresh foods after two hours at most.

Choosing a Cage Design

There is no such thing as a *perfect* cage, at least for the larger species of parrots. All cage designs seem to have their own strengths and weaknesses, and the choice of one design over another is really made after determining the lesser of two evils. For some, the purchase of a cage with a built-in "skirt" to contain the mess of seed inactivity, with disastrous health consequences. Ideally, the cage should be large enough for two perches, a third perch placed higher in the cage with enough headroom available for the parrot to roost on, and enough space to allow for tree branches (see Chapter Two for a partial listing of non-toxic varieties of tree branches for your parrot to gnaw on and enjoy ripping apart) and toys.

- **Perches.** The perches that you place in the cage should be of varying shapes, diameters, and textures, so that the bird's feet receive proper exercise. If a parrot spends most of its life standing on a few wooden dowels of uniform shape and diameter, it will be prone to developing lower limb joint and various orthopedic problems. Also, although the use of sandpaper covers for dowels of various uniform diameters is popular because they supposedly keep the bird's nails trimmed, I advise against their use. Parrots do not perch on the tips of their nails, but rather on the pads of their claws, and these pads are covered by tender and sensitive skin. A parrot that must stand on sandpaper all day long, every day, can develop a variety of skin sores on the underside of its claws. Pumice or cement perches are popular, but these materials, when overused, may also do more harm than good to parrots' feet. These perches appear to maintain trimmed nails perhaps

too well, potentially resulting in frequent falls and maybe even feather picking, especially with juvenile African Greys. If such a perch is used, it is recommended that it be placed by the water dish and not as the highest perch that is used at night for roosting.

- **Food and water bowls.** Make sure that food bowls are easily accessible from the outside of the cage, and that they are attached securely. Larger parrots will treat their food and water bowls as toys, and they are masters at being able to unhook them and toss them around.

The author is at home with his Hahn's Macaw. Notice how spacious the cage is for this miniature macaw. The jungle gym is constructed of manzanita wood.

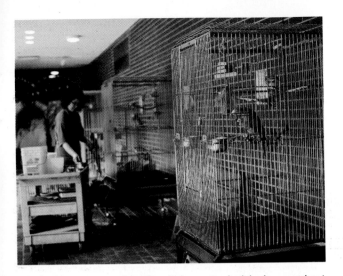

Dinnertime at the National Aviary. The cages are large, the food bowls are attached securely, and the parrots have access to mixed sunlight and shade.

bedding is newspaper. Newspapers are printed with soy-based inks that are nontoxic and biodegradable. They are inexpensive and easily removed and replaced. If you are offended by a particular article or advertisement, I highly recommend that you position it face up, under the metal grating at the bottom of the cage, and directly below the perch where your parrot roosts at night. You'll be pleased with the results the next morning.

- **Locks.** It is remarkable how adept the larger hookbills are at unfastening virtually all types of mechanisms used to keep cage doors closed. I have tried nuts and bolts, screws, and travel locks, with the result being that Zavi is entertained for a day or two while she figures out how to unscrew, unbolt, or bend the metal of a new lock. Fortunately, I have finally found a device that she has trouble opening, and I am able to pass this hard-won knowledge on to you: The answer is the caribeener used by rock climbers. This is a large metal safety clip that uses an internal spring mechanism; these terrific devices are available at backpacking and outdoor sports stores.

Cage Bedding

I have tried just about everything and I am convinced that the best

Toys and Swings

Most parrots—and especially the larger species—need to gnaw. This strong behavioral desire serves three very important purposes, partly because the beak is made of living, vascularized tissue that is well innervated by sensory nerves. This means that the beak is always growing, just as our fingernails are.

1. The parrot needs to keep its beak trimmed in order to maintain its usefulness for eating. If the beak becomes too overgrown, it becomes difficult if not impossible for the bird to use.

2. Because the beak has sensory receptors in it, the parrot is able to feel sensation through it, much the same way that we do with our hands and feet. That is why so many tame parrots, including my own, love to have their beaks gently scratched. It feels good.

3. Parrots love to gnaw because it is simply fun to chomp on, rip apart, tear, crush, shred, and destroy stuff. Watch any two-year-old human child who is left unsupervised in a home with lots of objects lying around and you'll see the same predictable phenomenon.

So, for these three reasons, birds just have to chew. Perhaps the last reason I listed is the most interesting: They want to chew because it is fun and interesting to do it.

Because parrots are able to appreciate the smoothness, roughness, hardness, softness, and temperature of objects by rubbing their beaks on them, they are equipped to explore their world by using their beak as an extra limb. Parrots are inquisitive, and they seem to constantly search for new ways to amuse themselves. If left without objects to gnaw on, toys to wrestle with and take apart, or other activities to busy themselves with, they easily become bored. In fact, boredom appears to be a common cause of feather plucking in parrots (see Chapter Seven). For this reason, toys need to be rotated fairly regularly, with new toys introduced from time to time. Many owners who leave their parrots home alone when they go to work each day also leave a radio turned on to combat boredom, and this is often quite helpful.

Remember that your parrot needs toys that are safe and nontoxic, and not easily destroyed. Many varieties

are available in pet shops and by mail order, and it is quite easy to make your own toys with chemically untreated pinewood available at lumberyards, and untreated leather that has been dyed only with vegetable colorings.

Killer, a Green Wing Macaw, is playing with his rope toy in the "marsh room" at the National Aviary.

Cleaning and Hygiene

In keeping a parrot in a home environment, you must provide fresh food and water *ad libitum;* that is, the parrot must have constant access to both food and water. By providing this, however, you are offering an open invitation to molds, mildew, bacteria, insects, rodents, and anything else on four, six, or eight legs that wants a snack. The best way to combat this onslaught of hungry life-forms is to keep your house, and especially the cage area, meticulously clean. Rather than exposing your bird to aerosol insecticides, try using sticky traps or flypaper placed out of reach of parrots and young children. If you ever require the services of an exterminator, remove your birds from the home before the application and keep them away for at least 24 hours after your home has been sprayed. Air out the home very well before your pets are brought back in.

Although your bird should be able to exercise its beak on perches and toys, but it should not be free to do so elsewhere around the house. Many old houses contain lead, which was widely used in the manufacture of electrical wiring, paints, solder, stained glass, ceramics, batteries, mirror backings, costume jewelry, and antique bird cages. Birds are highly susceptible to lead poisoning, as are humans, and you should check to make sure that your drinking water is not contaminated by lead from the water pipes or plumbing joints that are soldered with lead.

Baths and Showers

In the wild, your parrot may have taken baths several times a day, depending on the specific species and habitat; however, as a pet in your home, your bird's ability to take a bath or shower is completely out of its own control. It relies on you to help it take baths, which are essential to its overall health and well-being. During the bird's molt, these baths may be especially important, as they encourage the bird to preen. This intensive preening helps to remove loose feathers, feather sheaths, and particles of skin.

All that your parrot requires is a few opportunities a week to become thoroughly wet in lukewarm water, and to dry off by itself if it is warm outside, or with your gentle help if it is chilly out. As with anything else, it is best to introduce your parrot to the shower or bath slowly. If you treat the activity as a fun game, and be patient, you will be rewarded over time with a bird that sees this project the same way. Never force your bird's head under water, and do not get angry or upset—imagine being held against your will under a massive faucet. Finally, never use soaps, detergents, or shampoos while bathing your parrot. These cleaning agents are unnecessary and potentially toxic to your pet.

Air Quality

Although it is important to maintain a relatively constant temperature in your home, during the change of seasons, with proper insulation, heating, or air conditioning, keeping our birds in modern fuel-efficient homes creates problems. Not only are we sealing in heat or cool air, depending on the season, but we are sealing in a wide range of fumes and pollutants. Whenever possible, it is a good idea to open up a few windows in the home for a few minutes a day during the winter months, in order to allow in some fresh air; just make sure that your pet bird is not directly exposed to a blast of frigid air and that the windows are screened. Try to reduce the use of aerosol sprays as much as possible, and do not expose your pets to second-hand tobacco smoke.

It is a good idea to dust regularly. Also, it's advisable to invest in an electronic HEPA air filter to place in the room with the cage. This filter will pull airborne dust, pollutants, bacteria, and molds from the indoor atmosphere. Finally, it is well worth the price to install a carbon monoxide detector in the basement near your gas furnace. This relatively inexpensive device provides an early warning of carbon monoxide leakage into the home and could save not only your parrot's life, but your own as well. Always make sure that your heaters are in good working order, as both gas and kerosene heaters can emit carbon monoxide and nitrogen oxide. These odorless gases, if present in high quantities, may easily suffocate birds, humans, and any other air-breathing creature by depriving them of oxygen.

If you are moving into a new home with your bird, make sure that you check for the presence of high levels of radon, an odorless carcinogen. Often, in new homes you can

smell the presence of formaldehyde, a highly toxic chemical that is used in the manufacture of plywood, carpets, and curtains. If you do smell this, ventilate the home thoroughly, for 10 to 14 days, before your birds take up residence.

Moe, a Congo African Grey Parrot, is catching a few rays of sunshine.

Lighting

It is important to place the bird cage in a sunny room, so that the bird is exposed to broad-spectrum ultraviolet (UV) sunlight. This daily exposure to sunlight is important for several reasons:

1. Because parrots are diurnal animals, meaning that they are awake and forage for food during the daytime, they receive external cues from their environment that they use to help determine when it is time to be the most active in their search for food. In the wild, parrots appear to be the most active in feeding about one hour after sunrise, and again a about one hour before sunset. This is important for the pet bird owner to know because, if kept in a dimly lit room, your companion parrot may not eat enough food to survive.

2. Daily exposure to UV light is essential for the conversion of vitamin D, which is available from fresh red and orange vegetables, fruits, and vitamin supplements, into a form that is readily metabolized by the body. Without exposure to UV light, skin cells can not work to convert this vitamin into a more usable form (cholecalciferol), and the vitamin D will simply be passed, unused, through the body. If this happens to a serious extent, the parrot, and especially young, growing birds, will be prone to rickets, a very serious bone disease.

3. UV light acts as a natural disinfectant. It has a short wavelength that is a high-energy particle, effective in killing infectious microorganisms. Remember that UV light is blocked by glass and plexiglass. You need to keep this in mind when choosing a cage, and if you purchase one that includes glass, plexiglass, and/or plastic on all four sides, you will need to supplement with an indoor full-spectrum light that is mounted on the top of the cage, out of the bird's reach, of course.

For more about maintaining safe hygiene, the use of appropriate cleaning solutions and disinfectants, the provision of appropriate lighting, and the maintenance of good air quality, consult books by Lantermann and Alderton (see Useful Addresses and Literature, page 94).

Chapter Six
I'll Eat Almost Anything

The Omnivorous Parrot

Parrots, and most other birds, are generally omnivorous. That is, they'll eat almost anything. Some species of parrots, such as lories and lorikeets, have special dietary requirements. These particular species evolved with a brush-like tongue that helps them to more easily obtain nectar and pollen from flowering plants. Still, the majority of parrots, from the tiny budgerigars to the large macaws, are seed, nut, and fruit eaters.

Seeds

Feeding a seed diet to a parrot is not unlike feeding a person only bread and water. You would be able to survive for awhile on bread and water, but you wouldn't be too healthy, and you wouldn't live very long. Malnutrition, due to a limited diet typically restricted to seeds, is the single leading cause of disease and death in captive birds. An all-seed diet is high in fat, but low in vitamins, calcium, and just about everything else; thus, offering your

parrot a wide variety of nutritious foods, and taking the time to teach your bird to accept these foods, constitutes one of the best things you can do to help your pet live a long and healthy life. Before you attempt to make significant changes in your parrot's diet, it is important to have your pet examined by an avian veterinarian.

This Umbrella Cockatoo shares its owner's lunch.

time, despite claims to the contrary by seed distributors and extruded diet manufacturers.

The wide range of wild parrots' habitats is ecologically so diverse as to clearly indicate that different species have differing nutritional requirements. A parrot indigenous to the South American rainforest, such as a macaw, would have different food sources than would a cockatoo living in the open grasslands of central Australia. From the wide variety of pelleted diets available, it might be reasonable to initially purchase small amounts of a few brands and allow your parrot to choose. A combination mix of two or three brands might allow for the widest variety, but this diet base of extruded pellets should not provide more than 60 percent of the total caloric intake for the larger parrots, or more than 80 percent for the smaller species. Approximately 10 to 20 percent of a parrot's diet should consist of grains, seeds, breads, cereals, rices, and pasta. The remainder of a parrot's diet should consist of a combination of fresh fruit, vegetables, and animal protein.

Supplementing a parrot's pelleted diet is a simple matter, as a rich variety of choices that are nutritious and well-liked by most pet parrots probably already exists in your food pantry and refrigerator. One simple rule of thumb, however, is to allow your bird to share your food with you. There really are only a few foods that are dangerous, and should not be fed to your bird at all.

With many hundreds of hungry beaks to feed, meal preparation at a large aviary is a huge job every day.

Pelleted Diets

Over the past few years, extruded or pelleted diets have become increasingly popular. There are many brands to choose from, any of which would be a fine choice as the base of your parrot's diet, that is, the bottom and largest layer of the "food pyramid" for pet birds. Nonetheless, it is improper to regard the pelleted diet as a sole, nutritionally complete diet. The exact dietary needs of parrots remain undetermined at this

Parrots are prone to hardening of the arteries (atherosclerosis) and heart disease just as we are. The same rules apply, and the diet for most species of parrots should be low in fat and sodium. There are a few rare exceptions to this rule, such as the Hyacinth Macaw, a species that appears to require a relatively high fat content in its diet.

Do not feed your bird coffee, refined sugar, caffeinated beverages, chocolate, avocado, or dairy products. Small amounts of milk, such as on a piece of moist breakfast cereal, are fine; however, parrots are unable to digest the lactose sugar that is contained in most milk products. Hard cheese and yogurt contain less lactose, and are safer for your bird to have in moderation.

Safe Foods

Nuts, Grains, Seeds, Breads, Rices, and Pasta

Nuts, such as Brazil nuts and walnuts, are an excellent source of protein, but they also contain a considerable amount of fat. Nuts are wonderful treats, and for the larger parrots they are fun to crack open. Most parrots enjoy breads made from cornmeal with vegetables baked in. A bird breeder, long-time parrot owner, and friend, Lisa Zingsheim, offers her African Grey Seuss's favorite recipe for cornbread muffins.

The remainder of the diet should be designed to meet the nutritional

Seuss's Cornbread Muffins
Ingredients:
1 pkg. cornbread mix
1 can of creamed corn (low salt)
2 eggs, with shells
1 cup frozen vegetables, thawed
Directions:
Line the muffin tins with paper liners. Mix all ingredients together, making sure to crunch up the eggshells very well. Spoon mixture into muffin tins. Bake as directed on cornbread mix package, or until done (may take longer than package instructions). Freeze to keep; thaw as needed.

needs of the species of parrot that you own. Consult an avian veterinarian who can assist you in determining the proper proportions for each food group. For instance, small parrots such as budgerigars might prefer only vegetables and sprouted seeds, with an occasional piece of fruit. An Amazon Parrot or macaw might have a wider range of tastes for a variety of fruits and vegetables.

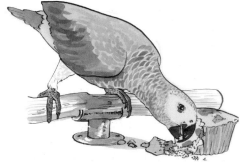

This African Grey devours a homemade muffin.

Benito, a Hyacinth Macaw, is munching on a Brazil nut.

Fruits

Recommended fruits include papaya, mango, banana, cherries, oranges, and apples. Apples, for example, are not only a good source for dietary fiber and pectin, but they also contain antibacterial, antiviral, and antiinflammatory agents. Papaya is valued for its high content of the digestive enzyme, papain, and its significant amount of beta-carotene. My birds love cherry tomatoes, which provide a valuable source of vitamin C.

Vegetables

Just about any vegetable is fair game, and most are great sources of fiber, vitamins, and other nutrients. Sweet potatoes are excellent sources of the antioxidant beta-carotene, which has been linked to the prevention of heart disease, cataracts, and various forms of cancer. Sweet potatoes are also an good source of fiber, and parrots generally love them. Other raw or boiled root vegetables, such as carrots and beets, are good for them as well.

Animal Proteins

Animal proteins include cheeses, water-packed tuna, hard-boiled or scrambled eggs, or a well-cooked chicken drumstick. Larger parrots might break the entire drumstick apart, cracking the bone to reach the marrow. Remember that these foods tend to spoil rapidly, so do not allow them to sit in the food dish for

Bean Vegetable Pasta Mix
Ingredients:
1 bag of 15 bean soup mix
1 bag of vegetable or other flavored pasta (try fun shapes)
1 bag of frozen vegetables or corn
For variety, add barley, chili peppers, or spices such as nutmeg or cinnamon.

Directions:
Soak the bean mix without the enclosed flavor packet in enough water to cover the beans, for two hours. Rinse, drain, and place back in the pot. Cover with fresh water, bring to a boil, and then simmer until beans are almost tender. Add pasta and cook until done. Drain excess water, mix in the frozen vegetables. Divide into individual servings in either ice cube trays or zip lock bags, and freeze. When ready to serve, thaw and heat in the microwave oven. Serve lukewarm.

more than a few hours, and make sure that any animal protein you offer as food has been well cooked.

Food Preparation and Time Management

Time is limited for all of us, and you can only spend so much of it worrying about your parrot's diet. Fortunately, there are several ways to make this important chore time efficient and otherwise painless. First of all, remember that with few exceptions, your table scraps from breakfast, lunch, and dinner are good food for your parrot. Second, several foods can be prepared well ahead of time and stored in the refrigerator or freezer in small, usable portions. For instance, vegetables can be precut for several day's worth of feedings, and a variety of pre-cut vegetables can be bought ready-to-go at the salad bar at many supermarkets. In fact, you might find a wide selection of vegetables that you wouldn't ordinarily think of purchasing. Remember to wash any vegetables or fruits before offering them to your bird. You can also purchase bags of frozen mixed vegetables, such as the pea/corn/carrot mix, and thaw out just the amount needed each day.

Many birds love warmed bean/pasta/vegetable mixes. You can make this delicious meal once or twice a month, and then freeze it in

separable portions, in sizes that your bird will consume in a few hours. For single birds, you can divide this mix into small portions using an ice cube tray—be careful to pull the correct ice cube tray out of your freezer when you decide to make yourself a mixed drink. A single portion can then be thawed and warmed in the microwave, but remember to check for uneven heating and hot spots.

On page 50 is a recipe for a bean vegetable pasta mix that can be made ahead of time, and frozen in individual serving size portions.

Variety is the key. Today's selection includes coconut, apple, blueberries, carrot, romaine lettuce, banana, and monkey biscuits.

Reforming the "Seed Junkie"

Birds do not possess a keen sense of smell, so they rely on their excellent eyesight to identify foods that they have tried before and know

Visual Preference

Some parrots take the visual preferences stuff just a little bit too far. A Quaker Parakeet named Delbert decided that when eating his pellet mix he simply hated the red ones. His owner wrote that, "when I change his food dish, it is completely cleaned out of the yellow and green pellets, but the red ones are all left in the bottom. Delbert also won't eat strawberries or tomatoes, or play with red toys. Recently, we bought a flame scallop for our saltwater tank, and he had a fit until we moved it to the side of the tank that he cannot see from his cage."

to be safe. Sometimes a parrot may learn to accept a new food after it has watched you try it yourself. Let your bird watch you eat the corn you are preparing, and be sure to tell your pet how yummy it is.

If your bird is hooked on dry seed, try buying a variety of quality seeds at your local health food store and soak them overnight. In the morning, pour off the excess water and sandwich your seeds between two layers of wet paper towel in a plastic container. Next, cover the container and place it in a dark closet or drawer for two days; ideally, the temperature should be between 65 and 75°F (18–24°C). Most of the seeds will begin to sprout, and these sprouting seeds, rich in antioxidants and other great substances, constitute a wonderful supplement to your parrot's diet.

Mixing a new food in small amounts with a food type that has already been well-accepted is another widely used method. As the bird tries the new food, gradually increase the amounts offered, while slowly decreasing the amount of the old food that you provide. You may also encounter great success in getting your parrot to accept a new food by changing the way in which it is prepared. A potato can be offered cooked, raw, grated, mashed, sliced, or carved to look like a flower. When my cockatiel was a baby, I fed her string cheese as a special treat. From that point forward, she would eat only vegetables that were sliced julienne style, that is, in thin strips. Even though she loved carrots, for instance, she wouldn't touch them if they were sliced in round sections; they had to be cut lengthwise. This might sound silly, but in the wild such particular likes and dislikes about a food's appearance is adaptive. Since a bird cannot recognize safe versus unsafe foods by smelling them to test for freshness, for instance, they learn to recognize the visual details of foods that they have safely eaten before.

Vitamin and Mineral Supplements

Your avian veterinarian is the most qualified individual to decide whether your parrot would benefit from any vitamin supplements. Generally speaking, a bird that is maintained on an assorted pellet diet that is generously supplemented with fresh fruits, vegetables, beans, grains, and small quantities of animal protein, should not require any other vitamin supplement; however, some species do require vitamin or mineral supplements. For instance, many breeders believe that African Greys should receive extra calcium, Fig Parrots require extra vitamin K, and Ecclectus Parrots require extra vitamin A. Again, it is wise to find a good avian veterinarian in your area, get to know him or her, have your bird examined yearly, and ask about whether your particular species of parrot requires any special dietary supplement(s).

Cuttlebones

One excellent way of supplying extra calcium as a dietary supplement, which is especially important to provide if you have a hen that is laying eggs, is to provide a cuttlebone that is clipped to the inside of the cage. A cuttlebone is the calcareous internal shell of a cuttlefish, a sea animal that is closely related to squids and octopi. Cuttlefish are found in oceans throughout the world, and cuttlebones may be purchased at almost any pet store that sells bird supplies. The cuttlebone

contains calcium carbonate, plus some other useful trace minerals. All birds require calcium, and cuttlebone is a great source for this essential mineral. Just as important, your parrot will love gnawing at it as it crunches and crumbles easily.

Dinnertime can be a terrific time to share with your feathered companion. It is heartwarming to watch a baby parrot learn to use its foot in a prehensile manner, to hold and manipulate food. Further, it is amazing to watch the incredible dexterity with which an adult parrot can skin a grape and if you are really lucky, share it with you.

Parrots should receive a variety of fresh fruit and vegetables every day. The selection should be changed from time to time to stimulate interest.

Chapter Seven

A Watchful Eye on Sickness and Disease

Preventive Medicine

In keeping with the well-founded idea that preventive medicine is more desirable than treating potentially life-threatening conditions on an emergency basis, I strongly recommend that you bring your companion bird to a qualified veterinarian once a year for a well-bird checkup. A regular physical examination to check your pet's growth and development, and nutritional health, including appropriate laboratory tests for the presence of bacterial, viral, or fungal infections, as well as various parasitic infestations, is well worth the investment of time and office fees. This chapter deals with simple steps to take in the home to prevent harmful accidents and disease, as well as household safety advice, and the major signs of illness to watch for.

I am unqualified to prepare a comprehensive chapter on avian veterinary medicine, with an appropriate treatment of the range of topics that are of concern to the amateur aviculturist. Several wonderful chapters and books on this subject are already available. In the Useful Addresses and Literature section, page 94, I have listed several of these, and I highly recommend that any responsible pet bird owner familiarize him- or herself with their contents. In addition, no amount of informally acquired knowledge on this subject will replace the important relationship that you should establish with a qualified avian veterinarian.

Follow These Rules to Good Health

If you follow these simple rules, you'll optimize your pet parrot's ability to enjoy a long, healthy life.

- Keep the cage and area in which the cage is placed very clean and free of insects, mice, and other vermin that may carry disease. Clean cages thoroughly and disinfect them on a regular basis, but make sure to remove all residue from the cleaning solutions themselves as a careful final step.

- Clean the food and water containers every time the contents are replaced. If you are using a water dish, rather than a bottle, the water in the open dish should be changed at least twice a day (morning and evening).
- Birds should not be exposed to extreme fluctuations in temperature, or any harsh weather conditions.
- Do not try to cut back on expenses by buying poor-quality seed or low-quality pellets.
- Do not place your bird in a stressful living situation. Provide a large cage with ample room for exercise, and do not house two parrots together if one dominates the other. Unless you are an experienced amateur aviculturist or breeder, and you know exactly what precautions to take, it is recommended that parrots be housed in separate cages. The cages may be kept close together, and parrots may share common play areas, such as a jungle gym, outside the cages if they have demonstrated a clear ability to get along with each other.
- Ask your avian veterinarian to show you how to determine if your bird is overweight. If your bird does become overweight, it is important to reduce the amount of fat in its diet. Remember that parrots are prone to the same atherosclerotic and heart diseases that we are.
- If you ever decide to keep more than one bird in your home, it is important to quarantine the new bird in a completely separate part of the house for 90 days. Preferably, the parrot in quarantine should be kept on a separate floor of your house. Make absolutely sure that you always wash your hands with a disinfectant soap before handling your other bird, its cage, or food dishes. During this period of quarantine—preferably before you bring the animal home or very soon thereafter—your new parrot should be thoroughly examined by an avian veterinarian.
- Keep your bird's wings and nails trimmed. This is discussed in greater detail on pages 61 and 62.
- Learn to recognize the early warning signs that your bird may be sick.

The Early Warning Signs of Illness

Parrots are prey animals in the wild. As a result, they have, over evolutionary time, developed the adaptive strategy of hiding any sickness or disease for as long as possible. This is adaptive because their natural predators attack sick or injured animals first, as they are easier to catch. In captivity, however, this instinctual behavior is problematic. It would be helpful to

This Military Macaw's eyes shine with good health.

us if our parrots would let us know, as soon as possible, when they are ill. As a bird owner it is important for you to learn to detect the earliest possible warning signs that suggest that your bird might be ill.

In her monograph *Parrots: Their Care and Breeding,* Rosemary Low mentions four basic warning signs to watch for that signal that a parrot may be ill:

- Sick birds often shut their eyes frequently "in the early stage of an illness before it has deteriorated to a stage where it is sleeping with its head tucked into the feathers of its mantle with both feet on the perch."
- The eyes may look dull, and in some cases, have a sunken appearance.
- The feathers, and especially those on the head, will appear ruffled.

- The droppings will appear unusual in both color and consistency; however, the droppings may change appearance depending on any alterations in the animal's diet. This, by itself, is not always suggestive of illness.

Although most parrots plant one foot on the perch with the other tucked up against their abdomen when they roost at night, some birds prefer to perch on two feet. Perching on two feet, by itself, is not suggestive of illness, but, if the eyes look dull or sunken, the animal is probably sick and should be examined by a veterinarian as soon as possible.

One unmistakable warning sign of serious illness is refusal to perch and preference for sitting and sleeping on the floor of its cage. Finally, most birds spend a great deal of time each day preening their feathers to make sure they are all lying correctly and free of dirt. Another warning sign of illness is that the bird stops preening and allows dirt, dust, oils, and droppings to remain on its plumage. Some sick birds stop eating, and require assisted feeding immediately by an experienced breeder or, more appropriately, an avian veterinarian. It is most important to carefully study and to learn your bird's normal behavior, at different times during the day and during different activities, so that you will be in the best possible position to quickly recognize abnormal behavioral signs of illness.

Bacterial, Viral, and Parasitic Illnesses

Parrots are susceptible to a broad range of bacterial, viral, and parasitic illnesses. An excellent selection of published resources reviews the diagnosis and treatment of these conditions. Especially useful are chapters by Rosemary Low and David Alderton (see page 94); following is a brief review of two of the more common conditions:

Psittacosis

Psittacosis, or parrot fever, ornithosis, or chlamydiosis, is caused by a bacterial organism called *Chlamydia psittaci*. Unfortunately, psittacosis is a common dis-

A home "hospital cage." Warmth and security are of prime importance to sick parrots.

ease in our domestic population of parrots. It is hard to detect because many parrots are carriers of this infectious disease, and clinical symptoms may appear only after the bird has had the illness for some time. Psittacosis affects many avian species, including canaries, pigeons, turkeys, doves, mynah birds, and parrots.

C. psittaci infests multiple organ systems. It is shed in dried feces, and other animals may become infected by inadvertently inhaling the organism that is present in aerosolized urine and respiratory secretions. Other sources of infection include bird bites, mouth-to-beak contact, and handling plumage or bodily tissues. Psittacosis is a zoonotic disease, which means that it is transmittable to people. Over the past decade, there have been more than 1,000 documented cases of

A cockatoo is receiving an oral antibiotic.

symptoms in people usually subside within 48 to 72 hours. Although human fatalities have occurred as a result of psittacosis, this is rare; fewer than one percent of individuals who are properly treated die from this infectious disease.

Although this illness is very difficult to detect in parrots, especially if the animal is acting as a carrier, early warning signs include respiratory distress and nasal or ocular discharge. Symptoms of chronic infection include weight loss, poor feathering, poor appetite, diarrhea, and lethargy. The presence of any of these warning signs should prompt you immediately to take your pet to an avian veterinarian who will need to perform a thorough physical examination, a complete blood cell count (CBC), a serum chemistry panel (SMA), a psittacosis antibody titer, a direct examination of a fecal sample, a psittacosis antigen test from the feces, cloaca, or a tissue sample, and a culture of the choana, crop, or cloaca. Affected birds are immediately put on antibiotic therapy.

You can develop a few simple habits that will reduce the likelihood that your parrot will become infected. First, whenever you visit a pet store or a friend's home and handle other birds, make sure that you wash your hands well with a disinfectant soap before you go home and handle your own pet. Second, whenever you purchase a new bird, make sure that you quarantine the animal and monitor it carefully for 90

human psittacosis reported in the United States. Not surprisingly, the largest single group of people affected by this bacterial infection were pet bird owners.

In humans, the incubation period varies from 5 to 14 days, and the symptoms are often referred to as "severe flulike symptoms," which include spiking fever, chills, headache, malaise, muscle soreness, and a bad cough. Oral antibiotics are effectively used to treat psittacosis, in both birds and people. With proper treatment, the days, before it is introduced to your other bird. This quarantine should be enforced even if the initial veterinary examination and laboratory tests were all normal. Finally, as mentioned throughout this book, practice careful hygiene and disinfect all cages, food and water dishes, toys, and all other cage and jungle gym items on a regular basis.

Psittacine Beak and Feather Disease (PBFD)

PBFD is a viral infection that is usually fatal in birds. Although young birds may die within six months to a year after the diagnosis is made, older birds may live for several years after developing the feather abnormalities and beak problems. This viral disease is not known to be zoonotic. It is easily diagnosed by a DNA test that identifies the virus in the bloodstream. When the blood sample is collected properly by a veterinarian, under sterile conditions and free of any surface contaminants on the skin, feathers, or nails, the test is extremely sensitive and accurate.

The biggest threat to the bird's health from PBFD results from the suppression of the animal's immune system. This leads to a vulnerability to opportunistic infections, and most birds die from secondary fungal, bacterial, other viral, or protozoal (parasitic) infections. The best analogy for PBFD would be the HIV virus in humans, in that both viruses lead to suppression of the immune system that causes the animal to become defenseless when exposed to other diseases.

Newly purchased birds should be routinely tested for PBFD. If the test is positive, the animal should be quarantined from other birds and then tested again in 90 days to see if the bird was able to fight off the infection. If the test is negative, then the bird may have successfully fought off the infection on its own. In this case, the bird should still be quarantined for another 90 days, with a third DNA blood test after this second quarantine period.

Hazards in the Home

In addition to hazards such as lead paint and predatory pets is the risk of crushing or suffocating your bird if it sleeps in your bed at night. Many small parrots, such as Conures, Miniature Macaws, and Senegal Parrots love to play under the covers and to snuggle up against their human companions to sleep. Although playtime under a blanket while you are awake can be fun, too many pets die each year as a result of their owners' desire to have them sleep under the covers with them at night. The potential for danger is clear: Parrots sleep at night just as we do, and they will not notice when you shift position while sleeping, or if another person climbs into bed and lies down on top of them by accident. Because

Trisha's Sad Story

I buried a young Senegal Parrot in my backyard this past summer for a grieving friend of mine. Trisha lives alone with her two sons, ages 8 and 11, and she was in the habit of bringing her Senegal Parrot into bed to sleep with her under the covers at night. One night, her youngest son climbed into bed with her in the middle of the night, and Trisha awoke the next morning to find that her parrot had been accidentally crushed and killed underneath her boy. This was her first parrot, and it was a tame and sweet bird. She mourned its loss for a few months, but she also learned a valuable lesson. Trisha is now a very responsible owner of a wonderful Hahn's Macaw baby that she learned to hand-feed herself.

your smaller parrot may weigh only 4 to 6 ounces (115–175g), and because it has such a fragile skeletal structure, it is all too easy to crush the animal during the night.

Another obvious household hazard is the risk of losing your bird through an open window or doorway if its wings are not clipped. There exists some serious disagreement about whether all pet parrots should have their wings clipped, but arguments in favor of this procedure are persuasive. Unless the bird is kept in a well-managed indoor or outdoor facility, such as zoos, breeding colonies, or at a major aviary such as the National Aviary in Pittsburgh, the wings should be clipped. With proper care, a parrot can get plenty of daily exercise without flying about the house, and, simply put, your captive-raised pet will not be able to survive if it accidentally escapes from the house and does not know how to forage for food and seek appropriate shelter. It is also initially easier to tame a bird if the flight feathers have been trimmed.

Care and Grooming

Clipping the Flight Feathers

The feather is not living tissue, and does not regenerate if it becomes worn or damaged. Birds compensate for this problem by periodically renewing their body covering; this is called a molt. A few large species, such as eagles and cranes, may retain some of their feathers for up to two years before they are replaced during a molt. Most birds, however, molt their feathers annually, and most replace the flight feathers on both wings in the same sequence and at the same time, to interfere as little as possible with their ability to fly. Because this is a natural process for the replacement of nonliving structures, the feathers do not contain any sensory receptors for pain, except at the very base of the feather quill, in the follicle buried in the skin. What this all means is that you can clip the flight feathers without causing the bird pain. The feathers will need to be clipped more than once a year to prevent flying, because the bird will continue to molt as usual, with new flight feathers growing in all the time. A strong, healthy parrot will be able to fly quite well with only two unclipped primary feathers on each wing. Although some people recommend leaving the outermost primary feather on each wing unclipped for cosmetic reasons, I have seen plenty of parrots—if they are frightened enough—fly quite effectively with just a single primary feather on each wing. My recommendation is to clip the outer five flight feathers on each wing, evenly and symmetrically. Use a large, sharp scissors to clip off two-thirds of the portion of the primary feathers that are visible below the next row of feathers that overlie the flight feathers, on the underside of the wing, called the *greater primary coverts*. If you cut much lower than this, you risk cutting into a blood vessel or preventing the bird from being able to properly regrow these feathers. When you clip the feathers, or nails, or trim the beak, always keep a small dish of clean cornstarch or baking flour nearby. If you cause any bleeding by accident, pack the wound with baking soda using the end of a cotton swab to stop the bleeding. This procedure may sound

The most radical wing trim. Outer seven primaries are cut short.

Potentially harmful trim leaves no support for blood feathers.

The least invasive trim offers protection for regrowing blood feathers.

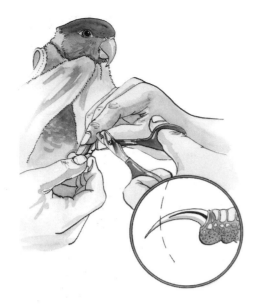

Trimming the Beak and Claws

Like our own fingernails, your parrot's beak and claws are living tissues, and they grow constantly. As a result, the beak may become overgrown, especially in species such as Senegal Parrots that grow the beak rapidly. For this reason, it is important to regularly check the upper mandible. The tip of the upper mandible may be trimmed with a nail clipper, but because the beak is well supplied by blood vessels, remove only a small bit of tissue from the very tip. Make sure that the tongue does not get in the way when you are about to make a cut. Again, before trying this yourself, have an experienced bird hobbyist, breeder, or veterinarian show you how.

The nails on the claws also will occasionally need trimming. When your parrot perches on your arm and it feels as if you are being pierced by eight needles, it is time to trim the claws. Each nail contains a vein that runs almost to the tip, and if the nail is cut too far back, bleeding can occur. You can see the vein if you hold the foot up to a light. Check to see where the vein ends before you begin trimming the nail. As with the flight feathers and beak, trimming the nails does not hurt the bird, but most birds are frightened by being restrained and having a foreign metal object, such as a nail clipper, thrust at them. There are right and wrong ways to perform this relatively simple procedure. So be sure to learn from an experienced person before attempting to do this on your own.

complicated, but it is actually quite simple. Just make sure that before attempting this yourself, you have an experienced individual show you how to do it properly.

Feather Plucking

There appear to be three major causes of feather plucking. Once a parrot develops this habit, it is very hard to break it, no matter what the original cause may have been. Although many birds are successfully cured of feather plucking by changes in their diet, cage, bathing opportunities, or social environment, it is better to prevent this behavior from developing than it is to try to stop

Causes of Feather Plucking

1. The first major cause of feather plucking is malnutrition or food allergies. Several nutrients, including vitamin A, various proteins, and calcium, are essential for normal feather growth and the maintenance of healthy skin. Despite

proper nutrition, some parrots seem to be allergic to certain foods or food additives, and the resulting skin irritation may lead to feather plucking in much the same way that we feel compelled to scratch a bad skin rash, sometimes to the point of bleeding.

Providing a variety of safe toys and exchanging them for new ones regularly is important for your parrot's mental health.

63

With proper nutrition, hygiene, lighting, bathing opportunities, an interesting environment, a sense of security, and social activities, your parrot's plumage will remain healthy and beautiful.

2. The second important cause of feather plucking is a lack of bathing opportunities. Although in northern climates we receive on average about 50 inches (127 cm) of rainfall a year, most natural habitats for tropical parrots receive from 100 to 350 inches (254–889 cm) of average rainfall a year. The bottom line is that the vast majority of our homes are too dry, especially during the winter months. Consider installing a home humidifier, attached to your furnace system, for use during the winter—preferably set at 30–35 percent relative humidity—but, regardless, make sure that your bird has an opportunity to bathe weekly, if not daily. Dry skin and inadequate access to full-spectrum UV lighting both contribute to impaired growth and maintenance of the feathers and skin,

making feather plucking more likely.

3. Finally, the third major reason for feather plucking may be summed up in one word: *boredom*. A significant portion of parrots that habitually pluck feathers do so for psychological reasons. Since parrots are intelligent and highly social animals, if they are left alone in a small cage for most of the day, with little access to the person they choose to pair-bond with and with few toys to occupy their interest, they will resort to removing feathers out of frustration and boredom. Many older parrots have also been known to suddenly begin feather plucking after many years of not doing so, if and when they experience an abrupt change in their living situation. If their owner passes away, they move to a new home, or a new person moves in, a parrot may feather pluck as a result of the new stress.

If your parrot begins to feather pluck, it is important to first bring the animal to an experienced avian veterinarian for a thorough medical examination. All possible causes need to be ruled out, including food allergies, malnutrition, parasitic infections, tapeworms (especially in the case of Australian species), the health of the skin and plumage, and the identification of any recent psychosocial stressors at home.

Chapter Eight
Establishing the Pecking Order

Introducing Your Parrot to Its New Home

When some parrots are first introduced to a new home, they want nothing more than to be cuddled and preened by their new human, but many birds are initially nervous and wary of their new surroundings. If this is the case, the most important thing you can do is to leave it alone. Do not make any initial attempts to handle the animal. Rather, place your new pet—in its cage—in the busiest part of the house so it can watch all the activity and slowly realize that the human occupants of the house do not mean it any harm. After a few days of adjustment, begin to spend more time near the cage and speak to the parrot softly and gently.

After a few weeks, the parrot will inevitably begin to show interest in its surroundings, and it will not appear to be as nervous. Now it is time to open the cage door and to allow the parrot to climb up to the top of its cage. Allow your new pet to explore its cage and any extra perches or play toys at its own pace. Do not try to force the bird to perch on your hand or arm, especially when it is just becoming used to the big world outside the cage.

Allow your parrot to investigate the world outside its cage at its own pace.

A bird will
attack when
it perceives
that another
is invading
its territory.

The bird should begin to view its cage as its own safe haven, and it is both expected and appropriate for the animal to try to defend its territory. Noted parrot authority Rosemary Low states that the "golden rule when taming a parrot is: Let it come to you." Although this method takes longer than trying to force a relationship, it will ultimately be more effective and satisfying because you are slowly building this human-parrot relationship on a foundation of mutual trust.

When the parrot finally decides that it is safe to approach you, it is best to initially pretend that the bird is not there; that is, make no sudden and potentially frightening movements. Once the animal realizes you do not intend to cause it any harm, and you are taking little notice that it is nearby, the parrot's innate curiosity will overwhelm it and the bird will rapidly become quite tame. At this point, it is time to allow it to perch on your hand and stroke it gently on the head.

Becoming Used to Your Hand

Even if your bird has been hand-fed as a baby, do not expect it immediately to understand that your hands are nonthreatening parts of your body. Think of this from the parrot's point of view: Your hands and fingers are a long distance from the head and trunk of your body so it is not immediately clear to the bird that your hand, which is extended several feet away from your head, actually belongs to you. The bird will, however, quickly learn to love you despite the fact that you have rather ugly-looking, long, featherless wings. When approaching any bird with your hand to give it a scratch or help preen away bits of feather sheath, always remember that parrots are prey animals—never stick out your hand to approach the bird from behind or from above. Your parrot may always remain somewhat nervous about being approached from behind or from above, and hand "petting," in the same way that we pet other animals, is not a normal activity for birds or any other prey species. Only predatory species approach other animals or their own young in this enveloping manner.

Your Parrot's Body Language

Learn to read a parrot's body language so that you are able to tell when it wants to have physical contact with you. For example, when a parrot dilates its pupils very

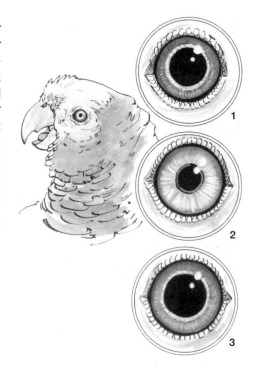

Expanding, dilating, and expanding the pupils in rapid succession, the parrot expresses agitation by "flashing."

abruptly—this is called "flashing"—it is either very excited to see you and is interested in what's going on, or it

Displaced Aggression

When my fiancee came to live with me, my Hahn's Macaw initially wanted nothing to do with her. In fact, when I would be holding the bird, and my fiancee would walk up to us, my bird would give me an angry nip as if to tell me "Stay away from that other woman; you're mine!" This behavior is not at all unusual, and it is something of which you should be careful. This behavior is known as *displaced aggression*, and it typi-cally occurs when your bird feels threatened by another person or animal that appears to be encroaching on its territory or interfering with its relationship with you, its chosen mate. This behavior is part of normal flock behavior in the wild, but in captivity it is a behavioral reaction that can hurt you quite badly. It is one of several reasons why it is important to not allow your parrot to perch on your shoulder and close to your eyes.

This Congo African Grey has developed a strong bond of trust with Jim Bonner, the Curator of Birds at the National Aviary.

interpret your parrot's various moods. Furthermore, as your bird becomes more adjusted to your home and its cage, and especially after it reaches sexual maturity, it will become more protective of its territory, which includes you as part of its territory, and less interested in being held or in any way touched by other strange humans with long, ugly, bald wings and fingers (see Chapter Three). This point cannot be stressed too much. If someone, especially a child, is bitten by your parrot after coming into your house and playing with your bird, the bird is not to blame; it is *your* fault.

Bringing Up Baby

Most new parrot owners initially purchase an immature bird that has already been weaned onto solid foods, but these same rules of the house should hold true for any new avian companion. First, as mentioned above, it is improper to allow your bird to habitually perch on your shoulder. Your eyes are very sensitive, and you only have two of them. Although you might feel that you are skilled at being able to quickly recognize changes in your bird's level of frustration, anxiety, or fear, one split second occurrence of displaced aggression and you might lose an eye. As hard as this would be to accept, this would again *not* be the bird's fault. Your parrot is a wild animal you have chosen to acclimate to your home

is warning you to stay away. If you have owned your parrot for awhile, and have developed a strong bond of trust with it, you will recognize that when it flashes its eyes at you, this will probably mean that it is excited to see you and that it wants your attention. If, however, you are trying to approach a strange parrot, at a pet store for example, and this bird flashes its eyes and perhaps bobs its head up and down, do not try to pet the bird unless you are prepared to lose a finger. Bear in mind that the larger parrots, such as the large macaws, can chomp down with roughly 700 pounds of pressure per square inch of their big beaks.

After you have owned a parrot for awhile, it becomes quite easy for you to be able to read your bird's body language, and to be able to anticipate when it is moody and behaving irritably. You must, however, assume that anyone who visits your home has no idea how to and lifestyle; it is not a domesticated animal such as a dog—and even dogs often behave unpredictably—that is more easily controlled around strangers or other perceived threats to their security.

In the wild, a parrot often demonstrates dominance over its flockmates by perching above them, that is, above the eye level of other parrots. In captivity, this same principal of establishing dominance holds true. With this piece of knowledge, you are well equipped to retain your position as the head of the household, and maintain a role of *nurturing dominance* over your pet. Simply put, if your parrot determines that it is the dominant animal in the relationship, then all your other attempts at controlling unwanted and potentially hazardous behaviors are doomed to failure. The first step then, is to place your parrot's cage, perches, jungle gym, and its own body, when you are holding it, below your eye level. Learn to provide a perch for your parrot on your hand that discourages climbing up to your shoulder. The best method has been described by Mattie Sue Athan in her 1993 book, *Guide to a Well-Behaved Parrot*. It is called the "Egyptian Grip."

What if My Bird Bites?

Despite the best efforts to train and establish dominance in a non-

Enjoy your parrot from eye level or below, without allowing it to perch on your shoulder.

threatening way, your bird will bite on occasion. Such occasional bites may not be intended as an attack, but merely as a means of gaining attention, showing displeasure, protecting territory, or as an attempt to reestablish its own dominance. In the early years of our relationship, my Blue and Gold Macaw, Zavi, nipped once in awhile but never in an attempt to physically hurt me. How do I know this? Because I still have all ten fingers and I have not lost any blood as a result of a nip. If she wanted to truly cause pain, it is well within her ability to do so. Of course, any biting is undesirable, and for many people—and especially for first-time parrot owners—biting for any reason is frightening.

It is, of course, best to try to prevent any biting behavior by attempting to understand what messages your bird is trying to communicate to you when it does bite. The first and most obvious reason for it to bite is because it is scared. It could be afraid of a new intruder in the home, it could be frightened of a particular color or shape that it despises, or it could be apprehensive because it was approached from above or from behind. A second reason for biting might be to protect its territory or its chosen mate from potential competition. Such competition might include other pets, your spouse, or your child. This urge to stake its territory and lay claim to its mate becomes much stronger in sexually mature parrots during the breeding season. This was discussed in greater detail in Chapter Three. This cyclical pattern of behavior is important to be aware of.

Biting and other obnoxious behavior in mature parrots may increase as a result of hormonal surges during the breeding season. Immature parrots may frequently bite for an entirely different set of reasons. Baby parrots quite often go through a teething stage, when they will test the edibility of just about anything. In addition, baby parrots instinctively grab their parent's beak to get attention, whether they want food, preening, warmth, or reassurance that everything is all right. If you are hand-raising a baby parrot, even after it has been weaned onto solid food, you have chosen to become its parent and your baby will want to use its beak to grab you for attention.

Finally, parrots are creatures of habit. They like their daily routines, and they do not to adapt well to abrupt changes in their schedules. You might feel that your pet is simply being grumpy, and no one has any clear idea whether they experience differing emotional states in the same manner that we do, but, regardless, your bird will let you know when it does not want to be forced to do something that alters, the daily rituals it anticipates. Never force your parrot to do something that frightens it or makes it nervous; this is the single best way to ruin the bond of trust that you have worked so hard to establish.

If your parrot misbehaves by biting or nipping on rare occasions, this does not spell disaster. Parrots sometimes act unpredictably, and seem to misbehave as if on purpose. What might start out as an initial misbehavior can easily become a habitual pattern, however. If you react poorly by yelling, screaming, shaking your finger at the bird, or performing similar antics, you are actually rewarding your bird for having bitten you in the first place. Your frazzled behavior, after having been bitten, will reward the parrot in two ways:

1. The bird will find your flailing about the room to be highly entertaining.

2. You'll be giving your bird extra attention in the process, which is probably what it wanted. As a result the bird will quickly learn the simple lesson that a strategically timed bite equals extra attention and lots of noise. This

can be prevented by not creating the chain of events that will lead the bird to feel that it is being rewarded for having misbehaved.

If your bird does give you an unwanted bite, remove your hand slowly and quietly, look the parrot straight in the eye and say "No biting." Then quietly walk away for a minute or two. Most of all, try to keep the drama to a minimum. *Never hit, throw, or drop the bird under any circumstances.* Birds, like elephants, seem to possess excellent memory capacity. Your bird will not forget that you have hit it, and the potential for long-term damage to the bond of trust is huge. Also, any violence on your part may either seriously injure the animal or cause the bird to become enraged, which would further worsen the situation.

Spoiling Baby

Just a few words are necessary about spoiling your new parrot with heaps of attention and affection, especially when it first joins your home and family. *Don't do it, or you'll be sorry!* This may seem like strange advice, as throughout this book I have reminded you that parrots are intelligent creatures that require the chance to bond with another bird or human, and the opportunity for regular social interaction, mutual preening, and play, but, I have also stressed that parrots tend to crave their regular daily routines, and these routines are established during the first weeks and months the bird is in your household.

If you and the rest of your family provide six to eight hours a day of attention to your new parrot, for example, over a summer vacation from school, what do you think might happen when your children return to school and you have to work full-time outside the home? Your parrot is simply not going to understand or readily accept this dramatic reduction in the amount of time it receives social contact each day. The long-term results of such spoiling, when all the attention is removed, can range from behavioral problems such as aggressive behavior, to feather plucking (see Chapter Seven). Although some families of parrots, such as cockatoos and African Greys, are known to be more susceptible to this problem than others seem to be, all parrots will respond poorly to dramatic changes in the amount of attention they receive. If you do not want your pet to act spoiled, do not spoil it in the first place. Set aside specific times in your daily routine—and this includes other family members who want to have a relationship with your parrot as well—to spend one-on-one time with your parrot, and your pet will soon come to expect this amount of quality time as part of its own daily schedule and, more important, it will learn to accept this amount of social time as both normal and appropriate.

How Do I Stop the Screaming?

This may be the most common question I receive from new parrot owners. As mentioned earlier (see page 30) parrots scream because they are able to do it, they are quite good at it, it may serve an important purpose from the bird's perspective at any given moment, and it may just be fun. Screaming may be especially fun if the bird can cause the humans in the house to make lots of noise as well, perhaps by getting them to yell back.

There are several behavioral techniques available to help train your bird not to scream. These methods fall into two categories: providing alternative sources of pleasure to halt the behavior, providing negative reinforcement to stop the behavior.

Alternative Sources of Pleasure

Providing alternative sources of pleasure whenever the bird screams, such as toys, favorite foods, and/or your undivided attention will certainly work in the short term; however, by doing this, you will rapidly train your parrot to learn that whenever it screams it will get something fun or comforting. This is the guaranteed method of training your bird to scream as much as possible.

Negative Reinforcement

In the field of psychology, the term *negative reinforcement* means to withhold a reward or action—that is, to not provide something that would ordinarily be provided. This is *not* the same thing as punishment. Remember: Under no circumstances should your parrot be punished, especially with physical means, to stop an unwanted behavior.

So how is negative reinforcement used appropriately? Although your parrot may scream for many different reasons, depending on the specific circumstance at the moment (for instance, your bird may scream on occasion because it is frightened by something or someone), most of the time parrots scream because they want attention. Remember that parrots are flock animals, and they are most comfortable when other members of their flock are nearby. In the dense forest canopy, other flockmates may not be easily visible, and so members of the flock spend a good portion of each day calling to each other to reassure one another that all is well. When you come home from your hard day at work, and spend time in part of the house that is physically removed from your parrot, your parrot will be unsettled by this physical distance and will call, talk, scream, or shriek for attention. It is even more upsetting to the bird if it can hear you walking or talking, but cannot see you.

When this occurs, first walk briefly into the room and speak quietly to your bird in order to assure it that you are here and safe. Then walk out of the room—this is the negative reinforcement part—and wait until the parrot has stopped screaming. Only after the bird has quieted down should you immediately return to the room and reward the animal by holding it, petting it, and talking softly to it. You will be surprised how quickly your parrot will learn two lessons from this behavior modification program: First, that when it screams you will leave the room and not return until it stops, and second, that when it does stop shrieking you will return to reward it with the attention and affection that it craves.

If your parrot does scream often, the behavioral modification technique that I have described will work, but only if you have ruled out other valid reasons for the bird's behavior that, if present, must be immediately addressed. First, a parrot that screams often may do so because it perceives danger, and it may be right. Do you have another pet, such as a large dog, that is antagonizing the bird? Do you have a young child who is mishandling the bird? Second, a parrot may be irritable and prone to scream when it is overtired and not able to get enough restful sleep. Parrots generally need as much sleep each day as there is darkness, at any given time of the year. In tropical regions of the world, this would amount to 10 to 12 hours of darkness throughout the year. Are you covering the cage at night and allowing your parrot to get enough restful sleep? Any experienced par-

rot owner will readily agree that it is fairly easy to tell when their birds are "wound up" from the day, acting irritable and grouchy—whether or not they actually experience that emotion is beside the point; they certainly act like they are cranky—and eager to return to their cage, have it covered with a bed sheet or other lightweight breathable cloth material, and to go to sleep.

Stopping Problems before They Start

When they feel safe in their environment, parrots are naturally inquisitive, playful, affectionate, and eager to learn. Specialty parrot shows at zoos and nature parks, at which individual birds are trained to perform tricks such as roller-skating or sinking miniature basketballs into miniature hoops are fun to watch because parrots are intelligent enough to learn the unexpected. As I describe in the next chapter, many parrots, depending on the species, are able to learn large vocabularies of human words and to form numerous associations among groups of words and specific behaviors, actions in the home, or possibly even specific emotional states. They do this because it leads to increased meaningful and positive social interactions with their chosen flockmates, such as their human companions, and because it is entertaining to them. Your bird is constantly observing and rehearsing your moves, behaviors, and speech sounds. It is looking to you for cues on how to behave properly.

A well-adjusted parrot that enjoys its regular schedule of individual attention, good nutrition, a safe home environment, restful sleep, and toys will be quite content to play by itself quietly for hours. My parrots do not bite me and they do not scream because they have learned that these behaviors will make it less likely that I will reward them with my attention or with treats. They step up on my hand when I ask them to, and my Hahn's Macaw is even somewhat potty trained, because I have patiently rehearsed these behaviors with them. No matter what you do, be patient, do not lose your temper, and do not use physical punishment to stop an unwanted behavior. Always remember that you have chosen to welcome an undomesticated animal into your heart and home. This is an unusual privilege.

Chapter Nine

Training Your Bird to Talk

Which types of parrots seem to learn best from the efforts of us, their adoptive humans, to train them to speak what sounds like our language? For that matter, why are they able to talk at all? Before we look at how to train our pets to say words or phrases, sing songs, or whistle a tune, let us first try to determine whether we are really talking about "language" when we speak of our parrots' vocal abilities.

Language or Memory?

Virtually all birds are capable of vocalization and even mimicry, especially those birds belonging to the order *Passeriformes*, the songbirds. Parrots, however, are among the relatively few families of birds that can acquire a large number of novel sounds that are not part of their native repertoire, in something of the same sense that human beings can learn how to speak words in a foreign language, even if we do not learn the *meaning* of those words.

The work of Dr. Irene Pepperberg has shown that, perhaps some, but not necessarily all types of parrots can be taught to attach abstract meaning to isolated types or categories of words or symbols. For instance, with much hard work and dedication, her famous African Grey Parrot, Alex, has been taught to understand and use arithmetical symbols to solve simple math problems. Alex is also able to perform simple multistep commands, such as "Put the blue key on the red square." Nonetheless, most parrots that live in our homes rather than in a laboratory and that learn large vocabularies of words—especially African Greys—do not learn new words in a manner that allows them to use them appropriately to convey completely new and unrehearsed abstract ideas, concerns, or wishes. Under usual circumstances parrots do not truly use human spoken language with proper grammar and syntax to communicate. While speaking, they do not evaluate the meaning of each word and how groups of words fit in different ways to express different ideas.

Classical Conditioning

If you were always to say the word "water" when it was time for a shower, your parrot would easily learn that it is probably time for a shower whenever it hears that particular word. In fact, it might learn to intentionally ask to take a shower, when it wants to, by saying "water." Similarly, your parrot might just as easily be taught that the phrase "No! Hot coffee!" means "Move your beak away from my hot mug of coffee." And so on. However, that same parrot would not immediately understand the meaning of a new sentence that it has never heard before, such as "You must first boil water to make hot coffee," even if it has formed clear associations between each of those words separately and their accompanying actions or behaviors.

A second example might be a parrot's seemingly appropriate use of the phrase "Don't worry" when it senses that its human companion is angry or upset. Although your parrot's use of this phrase might very well be appropriately timed, this would only occur if it has observed this phrase being used before in the household, either by you to console the bird, or by other family members who were upset. Thus, this process is really a fascinating case of *classical conditioning* rather than language. Through this process of classical conditioning, Max, a Congo African Grey from Glenshaw, Pennsylvania, has learned to say the word "Charge!" whenever he sees a football game on television.

I do not mean to suggest that parrots are not capable of effectively communicating their wishes or moods to us, with both intelligence and creativity; we all know that they certainly can and do. They are able to do so with a complex mixture of body language, such as raising a crest, or flashing their eyes, special calls and whistles that they teach us to mean different things, and the word-behavior associations that they have learned through this process of classical conditioning.

Classical conditioning, first eloquently described by the famous Russian physiologist, Ivan Pavlov, in his classic experiments with dogs, is a special form of memory. In our case, a parrot's speech is a demonstration of its keen ability to learn, rehearse, and memorize vocal calls that also happen to be human words. In the process of learning and memorizing these words, the animal may also form an association between a particular word or phrase such as water, with a specific behavior or object, such as taking a shower. In some recent scientific work I have argued that the size of an individual parrot's vocabulary is really a quantitative measure of its ability to memorize novel vocal calls and their associations, that is, an index of memorization ability. Of

Chico and the Weather

Some parrots form very complicated sets of associations between individual words and various events that take place around them. For example, Chico, a Congo African Grey from Prior Lake, Minnesota, has learned to use individual words properly to describe the weather outside. His owner writes that Chico "gives me a weather report every day...whether it's raining, snowing, sunny or a 'yucky day' (cloudy or foggy). One day we argued...he said that it was raining out and I said the sun was shining. I was working at my desk with my back to him and the window. After the third or fourth time, he said 'It's raining now, Mom!' and I got up to take a look.

We were having a sun shower and indeed it was raining."

Chico has also learned to ask questions of any new visitor, and he evidently expects an appropriate response. His owner wrote "One day I had an appointment with an auditor and Chico said, 'My name is Chico. What's your name?' The man ignored him and asked me where we could go to work. Chico asked again in a louder pitch, 'What's your name?!' I told the man that we could work at the dining room table. Just as we were leaving Chico's sight, he said, 'What's your name, *jerk*?!' I didn't know if I should laugh or cry, but the man finally said, 'My name is Timothy.' I often wonder what he thought."

course, this is an interesting and potentially useful behavioral measure for only those species that are able to speak in the first place. Vocabulary size wouldn't be a fair or valid measure of memory skills in cockatiels, for instance, a species of parrot that is not known to speak prolifically in the first place.

Which Parrots Are the Best Talkers?

One of the original purposes of my large survey study, from which this book arose, was to find out what types of parrots learn to talk best, that is, to develop large vocabularies of human words. To do this, we asked all pet owners who responded to our survey to tell us how many individual words their pets spoke. In fact, 64 of the 91 owners of African Greys provided detailed lists of up to 300 or more words. We also asked each owner to rate, on a three-point scale, how much "effort" they made in teaching their pet to talk (0 = no effort at all; 1 = modest effort, once or twice a week; 2 = much effort, such as daily practice sessions).

Although data were collected on 542 parrots in 1995–1996, I was not

Family	Sample Size	Average Number of Words	Range (least to most number of words)
Cockatoos	116	12	0–25
Macaws	51	14	0–202
Conures	59	12	0–114
African Greys	89	60	0–304
Amazons	82	34	0–410
Parakeets	66	10	0–90

able to look closely at several genera because of low sample sizes. For example, I had information only from 10 owners of Pionus, 29 owners of Poicephalus—and most of these birds were quite young—13 owners of Eclectus Parrots, and 34 owners of lories, lorikeets, and lovebirds. One reader of *Bird Talk* Magazine even sent me great information about his Kakariki (a small parakeet from New Zealand), which, by the way, was a six-month-old left-footed male that already spoke six words. Nonetheless, I had made a decision to look only at types of parrots for which I had data from at least 50 animals. With this limitation in mind, I found that vocabulary size varied considerably across various families of parrots.

No differences were found among five of the six parrot groups with respect to age; that is, the parrots in all these groups had an average age of four except for the Amazons, who had an average age of eight. Also, the data for vocabulary size, shown in the table above, were based on responses for all animals in each group, including very juvenile birds. In most cases, and across all families of parrots, individual birds under one year had much smaller vocabulary sizes—or they were unable to say any words at all—in comparison to older birds of the same type.

Which Parrots Respond Best to Training?

When I asked all individuals who participated in my survey to rate, on a three-point scale, how much effort they put into training their parrots to speak, I found an interesting relationship between training effort and lexicon size. The effort owners put into training cockatoos, including cockatiels, seemed to pay off the most. Moderate successes were found with Amazons and conures with increased training effort. Finally, no clear relationships between training effort and speaking ability were found for macaws, parakeets, and African Greys.

Wait a minute . . . African Greys?! How can this be true? Easily. With regard to the 89 African Greys, I found what is known among statisticians as a *ceiling effect*. That is, African Greys (both the Timneh and Congo subspecies) seem to be such natural talkers that all they really need is a comfortable home, a social and relaxed environment, and normal sounds and conversation. African Greys are so skilled at speaking that they will develop large vocabularies of human words if given only half a chance; no special effort to train them is required.

Of course, there are always exceptions to the rule that African Greys do not benefit much from intensive training efforts. Some individual owners of African Greys have found that extra hard work and dedication in training may pay off. A woman in Lancaster, Pennsylvania, works very hard to train her African Grey ". . . all the time . . . all day long. My Grey has a special smaller perch for talking, and we have one-hour talking and cuddling sessions each night between 9:00 and 10:00 P.M."

Parakeets also seem to show an ability to learn words that do not correlate significantly to increased training effort. Specifically, the 17 Grey-Cheeked Parakeets in my study (average age = 6.5 years; average number of words spoken = 13; range = 0–90) did not show any relationship between lexicon size and training effort, while the 24 Quaker Parakeets (average age = 3 years; average number of words spoken = 11; range = 0–50) did seem to respond "modestly" to training effort. Sometimes,

Maxwell's Sounds

Maxwell, a two-year-old Congo African Grey from Richmond, Virginia, has learned on his own to make sneezing sounds. He will continue to sneeze until someone says "Bless you, Maxwell," at which point he'll say "Thank you" and the sneezing will stop. Maxwell is also in the habit of waking his owners each morning by saying, "Open the pod bay door, please, Hal." This means that he wants his owners to come take him out of his cage in the morning. Both Maxwell and his owners are clearly science fiction fans who have enjoyed Stanley Kubrick's film, *2001: A Space Odyssey*, with the screenplay and novel by Arthur C. Clarke.

parakeets and other talking parrots find unusual household sounds to be particularly interesting. The owner of a Quaker Parakeet named Artex, from Astoria, New York, explained that "my soft-cushioned toilet seat must have a pinhole in it; when you sit on it air is let out of the pinhole, and Artex has chosen to imitate this sound."

Finally, the 51 macaws also seemed not to respond brilliantly to increased training efforts of any type, but for the opposite reason than the one found for the African Greys: The macaws showed what is known as a *floor effect*. Essentially, macaws are not terrific talkers, and no matter how much effort you put into training, they'll only talk if they want to, when they want to, and only with a few words of their choosing. As always, there are a few exceptions to this rule.

Up to this point, I have made a few general statements about the speaking ability of either separate genera or families of parrots. What about differing abilities among individual species within a given family? Let us first look at one family that, overall, responds quite minimally to training efforts—the macaws. On closer inspection, it seems that the two species that show absolutely no response to training effort are the Military and Severe Macaws. Blue and Gold Macaws respond a bit better to training, and Green-Wing Macaws respond even better still. Next, the 11 Hahn's Macaws and 7 Yellow-Naped Macaws (the "miniature macaws") seem to respond best to training efforts with humans, perhaps being rewarded with verbal praise or food, but still not nearly as well as do the Amazons or cockatoos. I did not have enough animals in this study to look separately at Scarlet, Hyacinth, or Lears Macaws.

Of the Amazon parrots, both the 10 Orange Wing and the 14 Mexican Double Yellow Head Parrots responded well to training, but the 15 Yellow-Naped and 7 Blue-Fronted Amazons were not brilliant students, although many of these parrots had large vocabularies. Overall, no differences were found with respect to training between male and female Amazons.

Now, what about the family that responded best to training? Which species had the worst and best word-learning students? Of all the Australasian parrots I was able to study, the 14 Lesser Sulphur-Crested and 16 Moluccan Cockatoos showed the least impressive response to training, but still a much better response than most parakeets, African Greys, or macaws. By comparison, the 35 Umbrella Cockatoos, 16 Goffin Cockatoos, and 25 cockatiels responded brilliantly to training efforts. Also, a pronounced sex difference was found among the cockatiels—the 14 females learned only one word, if any at all, whereas the 11 males learned an average of 6 words. The males that learned the most words—one male cockatiel spoke 22 words—were owned by humans who made strong efforts to train them to speak. I did not have enough animals in this study to look separately at Citron, Leadbeaters, Bare-Eyed, and Rose-Breasted Cockatoos.

How Large Can a Parrot's Vocabulary Get?

Whenever large databases that contain information obtained on hundreds of individual animals—in this case, 542 parrots—are subjected to statistical analyses, the goal is to search for reliable trends or patterns. Even if a statistical result is considered to be strong and reliable, we always assume that there are exceptions among individuals. After all, the objects of our study are living, intelligent, social, and highly complex creatures. For example, one Yellow-Collared Macaw was reported to have a vocabulary of 202 words, with the next runner-up, among the macaws, only speaking 58 words. This particular parrot, which must truly be an exceptional animal, was apparently the subject of intensive training efforts by his owner. This effort paid off, despite the fact that, as a general rule, macaws do not seem to respond terrifically to training. Among all families of parrots included in this study, rare exceptions to these general findings and conclusions were found, which is both normal and expected.

We know that, in humans, the capacity to continue to expand one's vocabulary continues throughout life, and no upper limit to the number of words that a human can possibly learn has yet been discerned. Alas, this does not seem to be the case for our parrots. There seems to be an upper limit to the number of words that even the most exceptional talkers, the African Greys, can learn. Most African Greys do not start to acquire substantial vocabularies until they are about one year old. After that, the learning curve (the rate at which the parrots expand their vocabulary sizes) for the 89 African Greys in my study showed a dramatic rise until about age 7, at which time even the best

talkers seemed to reach their peak. What I believe happens after this point is that African Greys—and other parrots as well—can certainly learn new words and phrases, but new words seem to replace old ones that are dropped because they have not been used for a long time.

Which Training Techniques Work Best?

I often see advertisements for home training materials that involve little or no time and effort on the part of humans who share our homes with feathered companions. It would be great to be able to just play a tape over and over while you are away at work, and after a few days or weeks of this, your parrot can miraculously speak. Unfortunately, many people have complained to me that these "quick fixes" that they purchased just don't seem to work as well as they thought they would. For example, an owner of an African Grey named Grendal wrote, "I have tried to teach him new words by leaving a radio on while I am gone. I also have purchased a compact disc that repeats words and phrases over and over again. However, Grendal still seems more intent on learning to make beeper sounds, microwave sounds, and telephone sounds."

In attempting to train a parrot this way, we are forgetting the one

Mimicking Sounds

My young Red-Sided Eclectus Parrot, Fergusson, is, after one week, already beginning to mimic the sounds of my Hahn's Macaw that lives in a separate cage in the same room. This is because he is forming a social bond with the macaw as they are now part of the same flock. The Eclectus is not, however, beginning to mimic the sounds of the hosts of the program 'All Things Considered' on National Public Radio, even though I turn on the radio each afternoon to listen to this program. My Eclectus Parrot is simply not as interested in forming a social bond with the voice of a radio announcer that is projected for him to hear from a rectangular metal box."

single reason why parrots speak in the first place—because it is a *social* activity, and parrots are highly *social* animals. Your parrot has no interest in forming a social bond with a tape recorder; rather, our feathered friends learn to mimic our speech sounds because they want our attention. Vocal communication is one principal means by which a parrot forms and maintains a social bond with others in its flock, ourselves included.

So what training techniques work best? Nothing can replace the quality time that you spend rehearsing new words with your parrot, in a relaxed atmosphere at home. For some inexplicable reason, I found that 18 parrot owners who participated in my survey had gone to great lengths to teach their pets to whistle the tune of the *Andy Griffith Show*. These data suggest that roughly 3.3 percent of domestically raised parrots are taught this television tune. The next runner-up for silly tunes was the opening to the television show, *Wheel of Fortune.*

Watch What You Say!

Be careful what you say around parrots that have demonstrated excellent abilities to acquire new vocabulary words. My parents knew of a couple in London who inherited an African Grey Parrot, whose original owners were in the process of getting a divorce. Apparently, the parrot had been privy to much arguing in the household, because it had learned several obscenities and it began to use them regularly in speech. After a few months of owning this parrot, the adoptive parents couldn't stand all the swearing any longer, but they were able to find a perfect solution to the problem. The parrot now lives at a residential care facility for geriatric patients, most of whom are hard of hearing and do not notice when the bird is sweetly, gently, and affectionately swearing at them.

In training your bird to talk, I recommend that you start rehearsing new words and phrases with your parrot while it is young, even if the animal is still a bit too young to necessarily repeat words yet. Speak in a pleasing and interesting voice, with much inflection (changes in pitch and tone). Repeat the chosen phrase over and over again, making good eye contact with your student. It seems that short training sessions of 5 to 10 minutes work well, and you should always reward the bird with an extra-special treat after each session. Most important, and to keep both you and your parrot from becoming frustrated with each other, maintain reasonable expectations. Not only do different species and genera of parrots show very differing levels of innate abilities to acquire vocabularies of human speech sounds, but individual animals—just like individual people—may be more or less innately talented at this skill.

With patience and practice, you may be rewarded with extra benefits that you had not initially anticipated.

One owner of a Timneh African Grey Parrot, in Vienna, Maryland, wrote that she has been comforted emotionally by her pet after her parents both passed away, as the bird continues to "carry on conversations between my mother and father, using each of their voices depending on which side of the conversation he's playing at any given time. He almost always still laughs in my dad's voice, which is kind of comforting." Once in awhile, this parrot will use the voice of his owner's father to ask "Do you want me?" The owner wrote that she responds by saying, "Yes, I want you . . . I love you." Once, after this verbal exchange took place a few times, the bird said (again, in the father's voice), "Are you talking to the bird?" Startled, its owner replied, "Yes, and to you too . . . I love you."

Chapter Ten

What Parrots Can Teach Us About Ourselves

In 1923, Dr. William T. Hornaday, the Director of the New York Zoological Park, wrote: "The feats of talking parrots and cockatoos, both in memory and expression, are really wonderful." Dr. Hornaday continued by listing, in descending order of ability, those species he thought the most skilled at talking, which he also considered to be a specialized form of memory functioning. This passage from the early 1920s reflects the long-held belief that parrots may hold a special place within the animal kingdom in that they possess unique cognitive and physical abilities that, if observed carefully, may teach us much about ourselves.

What Is Intelligence?

Perhaps the most compelling research questions for which the parrot may provide many of the answers are: What is intelligence?

How should intelligence be defined across species? How can intelligence best be measured? The noted psychologist, Dr. Robert J. Sternberg, has defined intelligence as "comprising the mental abilities necessary for adaptation to, as well as the selection and shaping of, any environmental context." Such a broad definition applies equally to parrot and human. Further, if one were to accept this as a reasonable definition of intelligence, then the parrot's demonstrated ability to learn new behaviors, to adapt to unfamiliar environments, and to shape its own method of interacting with new social surroundings leaves no room for disbelief. Parrots are, like humans, great apes, dogs, dolphins, porpoises, whales, and elephants, highly intelligent creatures.

Play Activity

One important characteristic of intelligent creatures is the capacity for boredom, and conversely, the desire to amuse themselves for pleasure and interest, without any discernible adaptive significance for the animal. It is well known that nonhuman primates, dolphins, elephants, and other intelligent creatures create and play with toys, probably to fight boredom. This is assumed because these behaviors are strikingly common and occur in the absence of any other tangible purpose, such as food gathering, sexual reproduction, locating shelter, or other necessities of life. How do we know that parrots use toys intelligently? Some might argue, for instance, that parrots use toys merely to chew and sharpen their beaks, or because they are simply attracted to the colored dyes that are used in the manufacture of bird toys. Such simple explanations are inadequate, however, when one meets a Blue-Crowned Conure like Bailey, who lives in Boyne City, Michigan. Bailey loves to "wrap himself up in new rope toys." Moreover, Bailey seems to especially like wooden blocks and, whenever he "is given a new wooden block, he likes to walk around for awhile with the wooden block balanced on his head." I'd like a skeptic of parrot intelligence to help me understand what the adaptive significance is for a Blue-Crowned Conure to walk around with a wooden block balanced on its head. In the absence of any better idea, I'll take a risk by surmising that this parrot may perform such a silly act because it is entertaining, interesting, and/or challenging.

Does Bailey "enjoy" this play activity? This is impossible to answer, as we have no method of inferring

whether parrots experience the same exact type and range of emotions that we are able to label with words such as "enjoy." However, it seems probable that if balancing a wooden block on his head was not pleasurable to Bailey, that is, if he didn't take interest in this activity, then he wouldn't do it in the first place.

Bailey enjoys balancing wooden blocks on his head, probably just for fun!

Perception and Expression of Emotion

Parrots may not share all the emotions that we do, but they clearly experience several of the basic ones such as fear, annoyance, and desire. In fact, they may well experience types of emotions that we, as human primates who are predatory and not prey animals, have no ability to comprehend ourselves. I would certainly agree that parrots are not able to discern the wide range of subtle differences in

Snoopy's Intelligence

Snoopy, a Congo African Grey from Sunnyside, New York, leaves little room for doubt that parrots can match up to Professor Sternberg's definition of intelligence (see page 84). Snoopy's owner described one incident, of the dozens that I had received from participants in my survey study, that shows off the parrot's ability to shape its own environment. "One time I was eating ice cream while Snoopy was sitting on my husband's shoulder. My husband was sitting on our love seat, and I was sitting right next to him on our couch. Snoopy saw me eating the ice cream and he walked down my husband's arm, then from one arm of the love seat to the arm of the couch, and then up my arm to my shoulder. I then handed the dish of ice cream to my husband, which prompted Snoopy to immediately return to my husband's shoulder. Once again, my husband handed the ice cream back to me. This time, Snoopy climbed down to the arm of the love seat, stopped in between the two of us, and waited to see which way the ice cream would go next."

Snoopy's owner also described a separate incident in which the parrot saw her husband eating jelly, and he wanted some too. "Snoopy saw that the jelly came from a jar, and so he made his way across the kitchen to get some. As he came close to the jar, we put the lid on and Snoopy immediately tried to pry it off. When that didn't work, he tried to unscrew it, and when that didn't work, he knocked the jar off the counter and looked down to see if anything would spill out."

human emotional tone that even we have trouble labeling with words— subtle differences in the perception and expression of ecstasy, elation, joy, glee, delight, bliss, happiness, contentment, and satisfaction. We all know that there is a difference between feeling elated versus feeling merely happy about an event; our parrots probably do not understand this difference. Still, this does not mean that they can't perceive our emotional states in a broad sense, just as we believe that we can perceive theirs. I, for one, am absolutely sure when my parrots are feeling frightened or annoyed.

There have been innumerable anecdotal reports of other types of animals, especially dogs, appearing to be sensitive to their owner's emotional states. The standard rule that if you approach a strange dog and you are frightened of it, then the dog will likely perceive your fear and may misbehave toward you is probably true. Can parrots correctly perceive at least a few of the broad categories of emotions that their owners might express? In the absence of reasonable experimental data to test this possibility, we must, for the time being, rely on anecdotal reports—and there are many such reports available. For example, the owner of Grey-Grey, an African Grey that lives in New Britain, Connecticut, says her pet seems to be able to identify specific types of emotions correctly. Grey-Grey's wings are clipped, and when he was young and tried to fly, his owner always responded by picking up the bird from the floor and saying, "Grey-Grey, are you okay?" with a concerned tone of voice. "Grey-Grey never repeated this phrase until one day, four years later, when I was watching a sad film on television and I started to cry for what I think was the first time in front of my parrot . . . I became aware of a soft voice from across the room repeatedly saying, 'Are you okay?' I turned around and Grey-Grey was watching me and repeating this to me softly until I stopped crying and went over to him."

Psychologists and other behavioral scientists are slowly beginning to accept the wealth of anecdotal and experimental evidence that shows that parrots, among other intelligent animals, have much to teach us about intelligence, creativity, and emotion.

Limb Preference (Footedness)

Parrots could be the single best animal to help us better understand why more than 80 percent of humans prefer to use their right hands for writing, drawing, throwing a ball, or picking up their feathered friends. They appear to be the only major vertebrates besides humans that show a strong inclination to use one "hand" over the other. Studies have found that parrots demonstrate almost the same percentage of left-footedness as humans do right-handedness. Although individual monkeys, dogs, apes, cats, or mice might show a strong preference for the right or left hand or paw, a strong preference is not readily apparent in large groups of these animals.

For more than 300 years, scientists studying the brain have focused on footedness in parrots. The first known study on the subject was published in 1647 by the British physician Sir Thomas Browne. Recently, the neuropsychologist Dr. Michael Corballis noted that foot preference in parrots constitutes "the most striking analogy to human handedness."

Parrot and Human Brain Asymmetries

Parrots have much to teach us about how our own brains are organized for motor control, learning and memory, perception, and maybe even the maintenance of emotional tone.

A parrot's preference for using one foot over another to eat a nut or grasp a toy is controlled by the brain, probably because one side of the brain exerts dominance over the

other side for controlling fine motor skills. Although we're not sure exactly how this works in birds, we know that the avian brain shows this kind of asymmetry for controlling other behaviors, such as visual perception, memory, fear, and courtship. By better understanding how these behaviors are managed by specific structures within the avian brain, we hope to learn more about how these same behaviors are managed by the human brain.

The parrot has been singularly important in helping us to better understand other mysteries of the brain, such as why the human brain is asymmetrically organized for many cognitive functions. For example, the left hemisphere of the brain, but not the right side, is primarily responsible for speech production in most righthanded persons. Patterns of cerebral asymmetry for brain control of cognitive functions such as speech, language, emotion, and memory tend to change when a person suffers from various types of brain diseases, so this phenomenon is important to study for clinical health care reasons; however, the question always remains as to why our brains are asymmetrically organized for these cognitive functions in the first place. How did this design for our brains originate?

Recently, I published data that showed that the vocabulary size in the African Grey Parrot is linked to motor asymmetries (footedness), and I described a neurobiological explanation for why this might be the case (see Snyder and Harris, Useful Addresses and Literature, page 94). These data suggests that the parrot brain, like our own brain, is asymmetrically organized for limb control as well as for memory functioning, in the same way that our own brains seem to be. If this is what these results mean, it is remarkable that such a similarity has been found in the parrot, since it is likely that birds branched off from the reptilian evolutionary line approximately 150,000,000 years ago. These recently uncovered parrot-human similarities in brain design may ultimately help us to better understand why the dominance of one brain hemisphere over another, for a given cognitive function, evolved in the first place.

The Future of Parrots and Humans

In her important monograph, *Parrots. Their Care and Breeding,* Rosemary Low describes the beliefs and priorities among aviculturists world-

This young boy isn't shy about hiding his amazement while watching a magnificent macaw.

wide at the turn of the twentieth century, which led to the extinction of the Carolina Parakeet. "By 1904, it was known that this conure was virtually extinct in the wild. Thousands of Carolina Conures had been imported to Europe and thousands more had been kept in captivity in the USA," and as the Marquess of Tavistock wrote in 1929, it could have been saved if "aviculturists had not been too lazy and unenterprising to make the effort." Low correctly points out that this same criticism holds true for the directors of zoos and aviaries at that time. The very last Carolina Conure, or parakeet as it has also been called, left this earth in February, 1918.

Conservationists have traditionally frowned on any emphasis on captive

*This pair of
Red-Headed
Conures are
part of a
formal captive
breeding
program.*

breeding as a means of conservation; however, that view has been changing, as once vast ecosystems have been lost to human population growth, pollution, deforestation, natural and man-made catastrophes, and poaching. The destruction of natural habitats for parrots and other birds is continuing at an alarming rate that is difficult for most people to imagine. Parrots, with their many specialized nutritional, shelter, breeding, and other requirements, are an appropriate bellwether with which to gauge how serious an environmental crisis we are now facing worldwide. Each year, several more species of parrots qualify for listing as endangered or critically endangered in the CITES treaty appendices.

Both professional and amateur aviculturists can do much to slow the rate of loss of critically endangered species, as already has been done for the Puerto Rican Amazon and the Thick-Billed Parrot.

Over the past few decades there have been impressive successes in captive breeding of both rare and common species of parrots. Domestic-bred parrots are now considered far more desirable as they are almost always sold as healthy babies that have been hand-fed and hand-tamed from the day they hatched. There are now several conservation programs that have the mission of reintroducing rare species of captive-bred parrots back into the wild. More than ten years have elapsed since Rosemary Low published her monograph (1986), one that has influenced me greatly. I agree that it remains "vitally important for all available parrot species to be established in captivity."

Glossary

Ad libitum To do something, such as eating or drinking, as much as is wanted and whenever desired.

Adaptive Able to improve or adjust in structure or habits, often through hereditary means, the manner in which an individual or a species interacts with its environment.

Antibody titer A laboratory test to detect the amount of an antibody in the blood. An antibody is a protein produced by white blood cells that either neutralizes or destroys foreign proteins, such as those from bacteria or viruses.

Antigen A protein that when introduced into the body stimulates the production of an antibody. Antigens include toxins, bacteria, foreign blood cells, and the cells of transplanted organs.

Antioxidants Agents that neutralize harmful free radicals in the body. Free radicals cause certain types of cancers and promote the formation of atherosclerosis.

Avian Pertaining to birds.

Aviary A large enclosure that is designed to hold birds in confinement, but that allows for proper exercise and social interaction.

Aviculture The care and breeding of birds.

Bacteria Specific types of microorganisms, most of which are capable of movement. Most bacteria derive their nourishment from organic material, and many varieties live as parasites on (or within) other living organisms. Some bacteria are necessary for normal bodily functions (e.g., digestion), whereas other bacteria produce poisonous substances that lead to a variety of illnesses.

Calcareous Containing lime (calcium oxide); chalky.

Carcinogen Any substance that precipitates cancerous growth.

Choana A funnel-shaped passage that connects the internal nares to the oral cavity.

Classical conditioning A process of behavior modification by which a subject comes to respond in a desired manner to a previously neutral stimulus that has been repeatedly presented along with an unconditioned stimulus that elicits the desired response.

Cloaca (From the Latin, meaning "sewer") This structure receives feces from the large intestine, urine from the kidneys, and eggs or sperm from the gonads, and opens to the exterior of the body through the vent.

Cognitive functions Mental processes or faculties, such as awareness, perception, memory, reasoning, and speech, that are controlled by the brain.

Complete blood count A laboratory test that evaluates the quantity and quality of red blood cells, white blood cells, and platelets. This test is used to diagnose conditions such as infection, anemia, and leukemia, among others.

Crop A permanent enlargement of the lower esophagus that is used for food storage.

Ecosystem A specific and reasonably well-defined combination of organisms (both plants and animals) and their physical environment.

Enzymes Special proteins that act as catalysts in the chemical changes that build up or break down basic living materials such as foods and complex sugars.

Feather sheath For feathers that grow after hatching, the feather is surrounded and protected temporarily by specialized types of skin cells that form a tough, rigid, protective tube.

Flight feathers Large and long feathers at the ends of each wing that are important for flight. The exposed portion of these feathers are curved slightly downward to maintain the aerodynamic shape of the wing.

Follicle Pit in the skin that contains specialized cells from which feathers grow.

Full spectrum light A light source that emits both visible and ultraviolet wavelengths of light (see Ultraviolet light).

Fungus (plural, *Fungi*) A division of plant-like organisms that includes molds and yeasts. Many forms cause illness or disease in plants and animals.

Genetic Diversity The variety of genetic information within a specific population of a species of animals or plants.

Gene pool The collective genetic information contained within a specific population of sexually reproducing organisms.

Genus (plural, *Genera*) The second lowest of six levels that form the binomial system of classification for all plants and animals, designed by the Swedish naturalist Carolus Linnaeus (1707–1778). The order of parrots, or *Psittaciformes*, is comprised of three separate genera (Parrots, Parakeets, and Macaws).

Immune system The body system that is composed of white blood cells, lymph nodes, the spleen, and the thalamus. The purpose of this system is to detect, neutralize, and destroy foreign proteins in the body.

Instinct The inheritance, in whole or in part, of specific key behaviors that are often particularly important for an animal's survival.

Lead poisoning A condition that results from chronic, repeated exposure to lead. Symptoms include abdominal pain, constipation, headache, and irritability. Early and severe exposure may lead to impairments in the development of the nervous system.

Lexicon A defined set of words; vocabulary.

Mimicry To copy or imitate closely, especially in speech, expression, and gesture.

Molt A periodic process of replacement of the outer body covering of feathers.

Neurodevelopmental Pertaining to the growth and development of the nervous system.

Order The third level in the Linnaean classification system (see *Genus*). There are 34 orders of birds (both living and extinct) in the class of *Aves*.

Parasite Any organism that requires another organism for its own life. A parasite may cause disease or death, or it may coexist with its host without causing harm.

Plumage The covering of feathers on a bird.

Poaching The act of illegally hunting, trapping, or fishing, often on protected property such as a game reserve.

Predatory Preying on other animals for food.

Preening The arrangement, cleaning, and general care of the feathers.

Prehensile To have one or more appendages, such as a hand, claw, or tail, that is designed for grasping or holding objects.

Prey animals An animal that is hunted by other animals for food.

Psittacine A bird that belongs to order *Psittaciformes*, and thus is a member of one of three genera of parrots.

Psittacosis antigen test A laboratory test that is designed to detect the presence of antigens for the Psittacosis virus (see Antigen).

Quarantine A period of time, during which an animal is kept separate and isolated in order to prevent the unintentional spread of a contagious disease.

Roost To rest or sleep on a perch.

Sensory nerves Nerve cells that are specialized to detect and transmit sensory information to the brain. Such information includes vision, touch, hearing, smells, and tastes.

Sensory receptors Specialized parts of the sensory nerves that directly receive the sensory information. For instance, there are different types of sensory receptors in the skin that are specialized to receive information about light, touch, heat, cold, vibration, and pain.

Serum chemistry panel A laboratory test that measures the level of electrolytes in the blood. This test is used to detect many metabolic, renal, endocrine, and gastrointestinal illnesses.

Species The basic unit of classification, following the binomial nomenclature developed by C. Linnaeus (see Genus). The three genera of parrots are comprised of approximately 315 distinct species.

Talon The claw of a bird.

Ultraviolet (UV) light Invisible radiation wavelengths from about 4 nanometers, on the border of the x-ray region, to about 380 nanometers, just beyond the violet range in the visible spectrum of light.

Upper mandible The upper portion of a bird's bill, or beak.

Vascularized Containing blood vessels. An area or organ that is well vascularized will bleed profusely if cut or damaged.

Virus A minute organism that is not visible with ordinary light microscopes. Viruses are parasitic and dependent on nutrients inside host cells for both metabolic and reproductive needs. Viruses cause a wide variety of infectious diseases in animals.

Useful Addresses and Literature

Books

Alderton, *The Complete Cage and Aviary Bird Handbook,* Bookmart Ltd., 1992.

Athan, *Guide to a Well-Behaved Parrot,* Barron's Educational Series, Hauppauge, New York, 1993.

Brooks, *On the Wing. The Life of Birds: From Feathers to Flight,* Charles Scribner's Sons, 1989.

Burgmann, *Feeding Your Pet Bird,* Barron's 1993.

Gallerstein, *Bird Owners' Home and Health Care,* Howell Book House, 1986.

Lantermann, *The New Parrot Handbook,* Barron's 1986.

Low, *Parrots: Their Care and Breeding,* Blandford Press, 1986.

Short, *The Lives of Birds of the World and Their Behavior,* Henry Holt and Co., 1993.

Skuych, *The Minds of Birds,* Texas A&M University Press, 1996.

Sparks, *Parrots. A Natural History,* Facts on File, Inc., 1990.

Magazines and Journal Articles

Bird Talk Magazine
P.O. Box 6050
Mission Viejo, CA 92690

Harris, L.J. "Footedness in Parrots," *Canadian Journal of Psychology,* 1989, **43,** 369–396.

Pepperberg, I. Birdspeak: "Squawking or Talking?" *Animal Kingdom, The Zoological Society Magazine,* 1983, 34–41.

Snyder P.J. and Harris L.J., "Lexicon Size and Its Relation to Foot Preference in the African Grey Parrot," *Neuropsychologia,* 1997, **35,** 919–926.

Snyder P.J., Harris L.J., Ceravolo N., and Bonner J., "Are Psittacines an Appropriate Model of Handedness In Humans?" *Brain and Cognition,* 1996, **32,** 208–211.

Organizations

American Federation of Aviculture
P.O. Box 56218l
Phoenix, AZ 85079

Internet Resources

http://www.aviary.org/home.html
http://www.ub.tu-clausthal.de/PAhtml/intro000.html

http://www.interaktv.com/BIRDS/Part.html

The National Aviary in Pittsburgh Home Page
The Online Book of Parrots, by H.-J. Pfeffer, Germany: General Introduction and Book Index
Parrots of the World: A Checklist. Compiled by Robert B. Hole, Jr.

A Scarlet Macaw enjoys a treat as its perchmate watches hopefully. Its bright plumage and endearing behavior make the Macaw one of the most popular avian companions. As the largest pet parrot, it needs plenty of living space. Smaller parrots that also delight their owners with talk and tricks are the Lory, Lorikeet, Conure, African Grey, and several other fascinating species that share the homes of parrot hobbyists.

Index

Aggression, displaced, 67–68
Air quality, 16, 44–45
Archaeopteryx, 3–5

Bacterial illnesses, 57–59
Bathing, 13–14, 44
Beaks, trimming, 62
Bedding, 42
Bird keeping, history, 5–6
Bites, 21, 69–71
Boarding, 22
Body language, 67–68
Bonding, 27–29
Boredom, 84–85
Bowls, 41, 55
Brain asymmetries, 88–89
Breads, 49
Breeding, importance, 30–31

Cages, 37–46
   design, 40–42
   location, 37–38
   size, 40–41
Care, daily, 21–22
Casserole, 32
Cats, interactions with, 34–36
Children, interactions with, 21
Classical conditioning, 76–77
Claws, trimming, 62
Cleanliness, 54–55
Companionship, 26–29
Confinement, 40
Confuciusornis sanctus, 4
Convention on International Trade
   in Endangered Species of
   Flora and Fauna (CITES), 6–8,
   89–90
Cornbread muffins, 49
Cuttlebones, 53

Diet, 15–16, 32, 47–53
   pellets, 48
Dog food, 32
Dogs, interactions with, 32–34
Dominance, 69

Ecotourism, 9–10
Emotion, 85–88
Endangered parrots, 8–11

Feather plucking, 63–64
Feeding, 32, 39–40, 47–53
   variety, 52–53
Ferrets, 35
Flashing, 67
Food:
   bowls, 41, 55
   preparation, 51–52
   safe, 49–51
Footedness, 88
Fruits, 50

Gnawing, 42–43
Grains, 49
Grooming, 13

Habitat, protecting, 10
Hand training, 66
Hazards, 16–21, 59–60
Health considerations, 54–64
History, 3–8
Homecoming, 65–66
Houseplants, 17–21
Housing, 37–46
Humidity, 39–40
Hygiene, 13, 43–44

Illness, symptoms, 55–57
Intelligence, 84–85

Kittens, interactions with,
   34–35

Language, 75
Lighting, 45–46
Limb preference, 88
Locks, 42

Malnutrition, 47
Memory, 75
Minerals, 53
Molt, 60

Negative reinforcement, 72–73
Noise, 21
Nuts, 49

Ownership considerations,
   12–24

Parasitic illnesses, 57–59
Parrot fever, 57–58
Pasta, 49
Pecking order, 65–74
Pellet foods, 48
Perches, 41
Pests, 8
Pet sitters, 22–23
Play, 84–85
Poaching, 6–8, 89–90
Protein, animal, 51
Psittacine Beak and Feather
   Disease, 59
Psittacosis, 57–58

Quarantine, 15, 55, 58–59

Rice, 49
Routine, 26, 71

Safety, 16–21
Screaming, 29–30,
   71–73
Seeds, 15–16, 47
Sexual maturation, 29
Showers, 13–14, 44
Social characteristics, 12,
   21–22
Supplements, 53
Swings, 42–43

Talking, training, 75–83
   breeds, 78–81
   techniques, 81–83
Temperature, 39–40, 55
Toxins, 16–19
Toys, 42–43

Vegetables, 50–51
Viral illnesses, 57–59
Vitamins, 53
Vocabulary, 77–78, 80–81

Water, 13–15, 43
   bowls, 41, 55
Weight, 55
Wing clipping, 60–62

Zoonotic diseases, 57–58